DESTINATION
Disneyland®
Resort with
DISABILITIES

GUIDEBOOK and PLANNER

for families and folks
with disabilities traveling
to Disneyland® Resort Park
and Disney California
Adventure® Park

Sue Buchholz and
Edna Wooldridge

NEW YORK

DESTINATION
Disneyland Resort® with Disabilities
A guidebook and planner for families and folks with disabilities traveling to Disneyland® Resort Park and Disney's California Adventure® Park

by Sue Buchholz and Edna Wooldridge

ISBN 978-1-60037-934-5 (Paperback)

Library of Congress Control Number: 2010943093

Published by:

MORGAN JAMES PUBLISHING
The Entrepreneurial Publisher
5 Penn Plaza, 23rd Floor
New York City, New York 10001
(212) 655-5470 Office
(516) 908-4496 Fax
www.MorganJamesPublishing.com

Cover Design by:
Rachel Lopez
rachel@r2cdesign.com

Interior Design by:
Bonnie Bushman
bbushman@bresnan.net

To Our Children

Sue's
Ty, Isabel, Carl, Anna, Dustin, & Teresa

Edna's
Lauren & Jenny

"There is more to life than increasing its speed."
Mahatma Gandhi

Credits

This book makes reference to various Disney copyrighted characters, trademarks, marks and registered marks owned by The Walt Disney Company and Disney Enterprises, Inc.

Edna and I want to thank our longtime friend and proofreader/editor Carol Ranney. This book would not have been possible without her hard work, patience, friendship and support.

Table of Contents

CHAPTER 4

Getting From the Airport to Your Hotel

CHAPTER 5

Getting from your hotel to Disneyland® Resort

CHAPTER 6

Overview of Disneyland® Resort

CHAPTER 7

Disneyland® Park Rides

CHAPTER 8
Disney's California Adventure® Park Rides

CHAPTER 9
Planning for the Child who has Autism or Sensory Integration Issues

Resources

Index

Preface

Our book is written to provide information for families and for people of all ages with disabilities. Disneyland® Resort includes Disneyland® Park, Disney's California Adventure® Park, and Downtown Disney® District. We believe Disneyland® Resort is a "magical" place where everyone can enjoy an escape. We have written our book as a guidebook and planner to make your vacation as stress free as possible. Throughout the book, we have chosen to use "he" over "he/she" for ease in reading. We have also attempted to be as politically correct as possible when addressing issues of disability.

The book is written in chronological order beginning with choosing a time of the year to travel, deciding how to travel, where to stay, and how to purchase Disney tickets ahead of time. We include checklists and information for getting your home, pets and plants ready for your trip. Packing lists and lists of items you may wish to ship ahead are included.

A chapter on flying with a link to Transportation Security Administration's (TSA) current guidelines is included. Basic tips on going through security are listed. We have also included a social story about plane travel and a social story about going through security. Both are at the end of Chapter 3. Getting from the airport to your hotel and getting from your hotel to Disneyland® Resort are next. Chapter 6 covers amenities offered inside Disneyland® Resort to make your visit the best ever, including guest relations and first aid areas. Chapters 7-8 cover the attractions in detail as far as accessibility and a description of each attraction. We include links to YouTube videos of each ride, which you can view ahead as you plan.

The final chapter covers preparation and adaptations for individuals with autism or sensory integration issues. These suggestions may also be helpful for any small child.

Resources are listed at the close of the book, and a Disneyland® Resort "Picture Communication Board" of the rides for folks with limited verbal skills is available for printing free of charge on our blog at http://Disneylandwithdisabilities.wordpress.com.

We have included Internet links and/or phone numbers for most of the information in our book so you can directly access resources, transportation, Disney information, TSA regulations and ride previews. We believe that good preparation and relevant information will allow you to be free to truly enjoy the magic.

Introduction

Imagine yourself at Disneyland® Resort, surrounded with the noise, color, and action of "The Happiest Place on Earth." Simultaneously you realize that the Maliboomer does what the guidebook says it does—shoots you 180 feet into the air in four seconds, then plunges you back down—and that your daughter has just gotten on it. So have a lot of other kids, but yours isn't clinging on for dear life—in fact she was born without arms, and your panicked mind envisions her shooting off into the stratosphere. She comes down, safe and sound, and is ready to do it again.

Remember those cute pastel teacups that go round and round? They look so mild. After you have your daughter maneuvered into place, over the saucer, into the cup, under the center wheel, you discover together that the gentle revolutions are a lot speedier and more nauseating than you could have imagined. Yet the two of you have just whizzed up and down in the Twilight Zone Tower of Terror and had a ball!

We've been there, and after numerous trips to Disneyland® Resort and Disney's California Adventure, I with my six and my longtime friend Edna with her two adopted special needs children, we decided that there should be a book written for people with disabilities to help them plan their trips to,

Lauren & the Mad Hatter

1

and adventures in, Disneyland˚ Resort. I also thought how nice it would be for wish granting organizations to be able to offer families this kind of information ahead of their trips.

Edna was more than willing to help or this book may never have come to fruition. Edna is far more organized and aware of details than I am. She and her daughter, Lauren, have been to Disneyland˚ Resort several times. Lauren would like to live there; she loves everything about it including the plane ride.

I, too, have traveled with various combinations of my six adopted children, to Disneyland˚ Resort Park and to Disney's California Adventure˚ Park. My children have a variety of challenges, and there were many things for each person to enjoy. The folks at Disneyland˚ Resort are striving to make the attractions more accessible for people with disabilities.

My oldest son, Ty, who had Reyes syndrome, and Edna's daughter, Jenny, who had Muscle-Eye-Brain Disease (MEB), have both passed away. They had each enjoyed a trip to Disneyland˚ Resort. Ty actually received a baseball cap from Mickey Mouse and is wearing it in Heaven. Ty enjoyed many of the faster rides; his favorite was the Matterhorn. Edna's precious adopted daughter, Jenny, received her wings in September 2007, at age 25. She went to Disneyland˚ Resort in 1990 and loved "it's a small world," and is now having the ride of her life in Heaven.

My youngest five children are first, Isabel, age 28, who has spina bifida, shunted hydrocephalus and was exposed to alcohol before birth. Isabel can walk with forearm crutches but does not have stamina for long distances. In the community she uses a small scooter and carries her crutches with her. She took her own scooter (a Pride Revo) and her crutches on the last trip. Isabel shares a home with several ladies who each need some assistance. She currently works at a movie theater as a ticket taker. We refer to her as the "bouncer" since she is responsible for checking age related identification.

Carl, age 23, has spina bifida. He has several shunts for hydrocephalus and is highly shunt dependent. He has some cognitive delays and a very severe latex allergy. Carl lives at home and does volunteer work. He has an outgoing personality and hopes to "work and get a paycheck like Isabel." He uses a manual wheelchair and is not able to stand for transfers.

Anna, 16, was born without arms but is totally independent in everything she wants to do. She is a bright student. During our recent trip to California she enjoyed touring Hollywood and seeing homes of the stars, and she had a great time at Disneyland® Resort.

Dustin, 12, has cerebral palsy, a severe hearing impairment, Pervasive Developmental Disorder and sensory integration issues. He is an independent walker, but tires easily and is prone to wander away from activities he doesn't care for. We took a lightweight folding transporter chair (15 pounds) with us for Dustin's use on our last trip.

Teresa, the youngest, is nine years old and is in fourth grade. She was also born without arms, and like Anna, is a foot user. She is a good student and is very outgoing except when it comes to meeting characters. She now boasts that she is not afraid of the princesses, but still shied away from Goofy, Pluto and even Mickey. I could not have successfully traveled to Disneyland® Resort last year with all five children without the assistance of my sister, Karen, and her daughter, Veronica.

Edna's daughter, Lauren, is almost 30 years old. She has Rett Syndrome and was able to walk independently until she developed Multiple Sclerosis. Lauren now walks with difficulty and uses a Zippie wheelchair when out of the home. Lauren and Edna last traveled to Disneyland® Resort for 16 days in October 2008. She lives at home with Edna, where she is cherished beyond cherishment.

This book contains the most up-to-date information available to us, as of summer 2010. Our obligatory disclaimer is that the folks at Disneyland® Resort can change their programs, hours of operation, attractions and restaurants, add new attractions and change or close others, etc. so some of the information in this book may not be current.

For questions you may need answered, we recommend you contact a "personal assistant" at Disneyland° Resort by calling 714-781-7290. Edna has called several times, and the personal assistant often called the specific attractions while Edna was on hold to get the needed answers. They are open 7 AM to 6 PM Pacific Time. The assistant encouraged Edna to phone back prior to their next visit so she can be updated on which attractions will be undergoing refurbishment and the hours of operation for Disneyland° Park and Disney's California Adventure Park° (the operating hours for each park differ). This information is also at the Disney website, http://Disneyland.disney.go.com.

All of us wish all of you a wonderful Disney adventure. Our hope is that this book will help make your vacation a bit more relaxing and loads of fun.

Sue and Edna

P.S. Before you leave, check out our blog for updated information. When you return, please share your insights so we can keep our book up-to-date. Our blog is at http://Disneylandwithdisabilities.wordpress.com.

sb & ew

CHAPTER 1

Planning Your Vacation to Disneyland® Resort

CHOOSING THE TIME OF YEAR

The first thing you may want to consider in anticipation of your Disneyland® Resort trip is the time of the year you want to travel. Many people choose summer because their children are on a break from school and the weather is nice. Remember, however, that almost EVERYONE has a summer vacation, and Southern California can be hot. Depending on any health issues associated with your disability, you may wish to travel at a time other than summer, when it may be cooler and the parks less crowded.

Let's explore the options, the general weather, the parks' hours of operation, and park attendance during the various seasons.

Winter: November to March:
Highs 68-73 degrees F.; Lows 42-52.

The weather is cooler in general and rain is possible. Our research has found that the three least crowded times in the year are:

- End of Thanksgiving Weekend to mid-December
- End of Labor Day Weekend to Columbus Day
- Second week of January to President's Day

Park hours are shorter in the winter months and some attractions may be closed for refurbishment. If a certain attraction or ride is important to your family, phone a personal assistant at 714-781-7290 to inquire. During the Christmas holidays there are carolers, a holiday parade, and holiday music and decorations.

Spring: April to June:
Highs 70-77 degrees F; Lows 53-60.

The spring weather is warmer, and the least crowded time begins two weeks after Easter Sunday and ends Memorial Day week. Spring break occurs over a six to seven week period depending on where you live around the country. Holy Week (the week leading up to Easter Sunday) is frequently a vacation week and one of the most crowded times at Disneyland˚ Resort.

Summer: End of school year until Labor Day:
Highs 77-87 degrees F; Lows 60-65.

The summer temperature is definitely warmer, and there is almost no chance of rain. The parks' hours of operation are the longest of the year, and attendance is the highest of any season.

Fall: Labor Day to Thanksgiving weekend:
Highs 73-81 degrees F; Lows 52-63.

With the exception of the Thanksgiving weekend (Thursday through Sunday), there are low to average crowds. Our research indicates that the temperature in October is in the 70s. Edna and Lauren go in October and the temperature has always been in the 90s—usually the high 90s. Edna spoke to several Cast Members (Disneyland˚ Resort employees are referred to as Cast Members) who said the temperature in October is usually in the 90s due to the Santa Ana winds.

TIP: Saturdays are almost always crowded, year round.

HOW WILL YOU TRAVEL TO ANAHEIM?

You may drive, take the train, or fly to Disneyland˚ Resort. Since most people will be flying, air travel is covered most extensively here.

Driving

If you drive, you will definitely want a map of the area. You can plan your travel ahead with maps from the following websites:

http://maps.google.com

www.mapquest.com

http://maps.yahoo.com

Automobile clubs, such as AAA and CAA (Canadian Automobile Association) offer free state and city maps. AAA prints a travel guide of Southern California that includes Las Vegas; it is free to AAA members. It lists the hotels and motels in the area and information about such. www.aaa.com

Southern California streets and freeways can be quite busy during rush hours, which can double your travel time through LA and vicinity. Some general California driving laws include:

- Seat belts are required for all passengers in the front and back seats.
- Right turns are allowed at red lights unless otherwise posted.
- Pedestrians have the right-of-way at crosswalks.
- U-turns are allowed at intersections unless otherwise posted.

Check http://www.caldrive.com/law.html or http://www.dmv.ca.gov for California laws specifically for the traveler. It includes child safety restraint and cell phone use laws as well.

By Train
(Metrolink trains and Amtrak serve the Anaheim station)

Metrolink commuter service, 800 371-5465 or www.metrolinktrains.com

Amtrak can be reached at 800 872-7245 or www.amtrak.com

http://www.metrolinktrains.com/stations/detail.php?id=81 (direct link to their Anaheim station)

The train station is located at 2150 East Katella Avenue, which is about two miles from Disneyland˚ Resort. A taxicab from the train station to Disneyland˚ Resort is about $17 each way. Yellow Cab is the official cab serving Anaheim. They can be reached at 800-535-2211. Orange County Transportation Authority (OCTA) buses also serve the station. http://www.octa.net/

By Plane

Choosing an airport. There are three serving the area:

- Los Angeles International Airport (LAX) is one of the world's busiest airports and is approximately 45 minutes from Anaheim. LAX serves more than 70 commercial airlines.

- Orange County's John Wayne Airport (SNA) is about 30 minutes from Anaheim. It is served by 11 commercial airlines. It may not be possible to get a direct flight to SNA depending on where your flight originates. It is a smaller airport, which makes it easier to navigate. For this reason, Edna prefers SNA.

- Long Beach Airport (LGB) is also near Anaheim. Fewer airlines serve LGB with non-stop flights.

If you use a travel agent to plan your entire trip, make sure the agent comes well recommended by someone you know who has a disability. You can plan your own flight by phoning individual airlines to make reservations and ask questions.

Another alternative is to go online and use a service like www.cheapflights.com where you can compare prices and availability of flights and airlines from a number of different airlines and services (American Airlines, Orbitz, Expedia, Travelocity and more), all from one site. Cheapflights offers a number of accessibility options such as large font on their website. You can then click across to the recommended site of your choice, where your dates and other information have been transferred, to check flights and make reservations.

Guidelines for making online reservations

- Try to book early. The price of fuel is driving airline costs up.

- If you require bulkhead seating for your child or to accommodate your disability, you should request that early on.

- Be sure to let the airline know if you are using oxygen.

- Read all the information concerning refunds or costs involved if you should need to cancel or rebook your flight.

- It can be difficult or impossible to select bulkhead seating or another seat with extra legroom online; you will need to phone the airline directly with your request. Some airlines may connect you to reservations sales agents in other countries.

For this recent trip Sue booked online with United Airlines. United's online reservations site asked about specific needs of travelers with physical challenges. Sue still needed to call to get seats closer to the front of the plane for Carl and Isabel; she was connected to a gentleman in India who was able to change the seating.

Edna prefers Alaska Airlines. (Edna's note: We use non-stop flights with Alaska Airlines and I call the airline directly to make reservations and let them know the exact seats we need. While Lauren loves flying, I prefer the shortest possible flight. Alaska Airlines is very accommodating to people who have disabilities. When we took Jenny with us we attached her feeding bag to the overhead compartment so she could get her tube feeding during the flight. A pilot carried Jenny's equipment into the airport. We have many examples of their helpfulness.)

- Plan connections with extra time in mind, especially if you will need to wait for a wheelchair or the plane's aisle chair. If you are connecting to a different airline or need to change terminals in a large airport you will need the extra time.

- Currently, it is possible to print your e-ticket boarding passes within 24 hours of your flight boarding time. This saved some time for Sue and her family. There was no need to print out eight tickets/boarding passes at the airport. The hotel had Internet access and allowed us to do this for the return tickets as well.

Most airlines allow people with disabilities and families with small children to board first, and have those with physical disabilities get off the plane last. This is especially true if you are waiting for your own wheelchair or scooter to be brought to the plane and/or if you require the plane's aisle chair.

WHERE WILL YOU STAY?

There are three general ways of looking at lodging in Anaheim. One, you can stay in the park at one of Disneyland® Resort's three hotels: Disneyland® Hotel, Disney's Paradise Pier® Hotel or Disney's Grand Californian Hotel®. All three offer accommodations for the disabled. Disneyland® Resort hotels are more expensive than are accommodations outside of the park and the prices remain the same year round. For information go to www.Disneyland.com and click on Places to Stay.

Two, you can stay outside the park in less expensive lodging but close enough to walk, or three, you can stay outside the park and drive or use other transportation to get to the park. There are motels and hotels, inns and suites of every size, shape, location, and price in the Anaheim area. As mentioned earlier, the AAA book for Southern California lists accommodations in the Anaheim area, their amenities, general pricing guidelines and phone numbers to reach individual hotels.

Orange County Visitor's Bureau has a website that lists hotels and their addresses, and you can press the "details" button of any hotel on the list and there is a button to bring up a map of where the hotel is located. Their website is http://www.anaheimoc.org/.

Phoning the hotel directly is better than speaking to someone at the corporate office of a hotel chain if you have specific questions. Many have toll free numbers, although some do not. Sometimes the lodging section in the AAA book is unintentionally misleading. A "block" near Disneyland® Resort may mean one very long block from the boundary of Disneyland® Resort, where you then continue your trek for an even longer walk to reach the actual entrance. Likewise, not all the specific information you may need is in the AAA book or on the specific website. Lodging near Disneyland® Resort undergoes refurbishment from time to time.

For their recent trip, Sue chose one of the hotels on Harbor Blvd. directly across the street from the East Shuttle entrance because she wanted to walk to Disneyland® Resort. With three kids in wheelchairs she did not want to load and unload chairs onto a shuttle every time they needed to come and go from the park. The hotel was right across Harbor from the entrance and near several restaurants, mini marts and fast food establishments. It was a perfect location for her family. The hotel did not assist with luggage and did not store luggage until the room opened (they had to haul their luggage to coin operated lockers in the hotel for storage until the room was ready.) This hotel did have their boxes of items sent by UPS waiting. Sue had to carry them up to the room herself.

All the hotels Edna and Lauren have stayed in have had their boxes of supplies waiting for them and the concierge took them to the room. Lauren likes riding a bus or shuttle from the hotel to Disneyland® Resort so Edna books a hotel a bit further away on Harbor Blvd. We suggest you call several hotels and ask many questions:

- Do you honor AAA or other special rates?
- What type of door key do you have?
- Is there a safe in the room and is there an extra charge for using it? If there isn't a room safe, is there one at the front desk?

- Is there concierge service? Does the hotel offer assistance with luggage?

- What are the check in and checkout times?

- Do you have wheelchair accessible rooms?

- Does the accessible room have a shower, tub, roll in shower, shower seat, hand held sprayer, etc?

- How many of the rooms are non-smoking ones? Some hotels are now smoke free establishments. If you stay in a hotel that has both smoking and non-smoking rooms and you are allergic, request a room as far from the smoking rooms as possible.

- Is there an elevator? This many seem redundant, but some motels with more than one floor do not have an elevator.

- Is there parking, and if so, is there an extra charge?

- Is there a coin laundry on the premises?

- Does the hotel offer its own transportation service to Disneyland˚ Resort, and if so, does the shuttle have a lift for wheelchairs? This is a crucial question since some hotels have their own shuttles, but those shuttles are usually not wheelchair accessible and do not have lifts. The Howard Johnson has a cute trolley that a wheelchair can fit on, but one has to carry the wheelchair and child into the trolley. Lauren loved that trolley so much when she was small, but she would not be able to get into it now.

- Do they provide Braille or large print information?

- Is there TDD/TTY service?

- Do the smoke detectors have strobe lights?

- How are the beds arranged? Is there space to transfer? Can you move beds?

- Do they allow service dogs? If you are allergic be sure to request a room that hasn't had a service animal in it.

- Is there a swimming pool and is the pool accessible? Is it an indoor or outdoor pool? Is it heated? What temperature?

- Is there an exercise room?

- Is there a microwave? A refrigerator? An iron? (Edna irons; Sue doesn't need an iron very often.)

- Has the hotel recently had renovations done? This is a crucial question if you have chemical allergies.

- Do they offer a breakfast plan with lodging? If so, what does the breakfast include? Is it a continental or full breakfast?

- If they do not offer breakfast, are there restaurants nearby?

- Does the hotel sell Disney admission tickets? How much are they? Sue bought her tickets online, printed out a barcode "ticket" for each one and just took everyone to the turnstile where an actual ticket was given for each barcode "ticket." They bought five-day Park Hopper® tickets that were on sale for the price of a three-day ticket. The hotel sold the same tickets for $5.00 more per ticket.

Very important question: Can I ship items ahead?

Despite the fact that Sue and family had to "cram" their luggage into lockers at their hotel to await the room being readied, the hotel didn't bat an eye about receiving and storing items for them until they arrived. Most hotels will accept packages/boxes but request they not arrive more than one week prior to your arrival. UPS shipped Sue's three boxes of supplies for around $50 and the boxes arrived four days before they did. With UPS and other delivery services, you can track your packages. Their schedules are fairly precise as to how long it will take your items to reach their destination. Edna's UPS shipping list is at the beginning of Chapter 2.

PURCHASING DISNEYLAND® RESORT ADMISSION TICKETS

You can purchase Disney admission tickets ahead of time or wait until you arrive at Disneyland® Resort to do this. If you are traveling at a busy time of the year, it will save you time if you get your tickets ahead, especially if you know in advance how long you will be visiting.

You can purchase a 1-Day 1-Park ticket to either Disneyland® Park or Disney's California Adventure® Park. There are Park Hopper® tickets which allow you to move back and forth between Disneyland® Park and Disney's California Adventure® Park as many times as you want in a day. The entrance to Disneyland® Park is directly across from Disney's California Adventure® Park, with a plaza in between. Moving from one park to the other is very easy.

Disney also sells annual passes. The Premium Annual Pass does not have blackout dates and is good for an entire year. It also has "perks" like free parking. It may be worth your while to purchase one if you are going to use the parking garage and plan to be there for five or more days. You can purchase the annual passes at Disney stores and have them validated at Disneyland® Resort. Your photo will be taken and placed on the pass. Edna and Lauren always stay so long that they purchase annual passes, since it is more economical.

The Deluxe Annual Pass is good for 315 days, so there are a few blackout dates, but if you will be at Disneyland® Resort for more than seven days the Deluxe Annual Pass is a good deal. Parking is not included.

You can also purchase a Southern California Pass which includes a three day Disneyland® Resort Park Hopper Disneyland® Resort Bonus Ticket and admission to Universal Studios Hollywood®, Sea World® (San Diego) and either the San Diego Zoo® or the San Diego Wild Animal Park®. This is a great bargain if you plan to see these other Southern California attractions.

Check out the prices online, even if you choose to buy later.

Tickets are available at the following:

- Disneyland® Resort ticket booths
- By phone order using a personal check or money order at 714-781-4400
- By phone with a debit or credit card at 714-781-4043
- Online with two options: you can have them mailed to you for a handling fee, or you can print them yourself online and exchange the

online bar-coded "tickets" for real tickets at the turnstile entrance. (Sue's family did this without any trouble.) Find online tickets at http://disneylandchanged.disney.go.com/tickets/

- By mail. You must allow processing time, so order early. Send a personal check or money order and a $10 handling fee for orders over $200 to: Disneyland˚ Resort Ticket Mail Order Services. Box 61061, Anaheim, CA 92803

- AAA sells Disneyland˚ Resort tickets in their offices. Phone first to make sure they have some on hand.

- Disney Stores nationwide sell Disneyland˚ Resort tickets

OTHER MISCELLANEOUS, BUT IMPORTANT THINGS YOU MAY WANT TO CONSIDER EARLY IN YOUR PLANNING.

If the disabled person traveling with you receives a new medical card every month, and they have serious medical issues for which the card may be needed, you may want to plan your trip around having the card with you. If a trusted neighbor or friend is getting your mail, you can ask that person to FAX you a copy when it arrives.

If peanut allergies are a problem for your family, call the airline ahead to see if peanuts are still served on the flights.

Edna always takes Lauren to the doctor prior to leaving to have her ears checked and make sure she is without infection, and also gets any letters she may need concerning Lauren's medical condition. She suggests checking with your doctor before leaving if you or your child might be susceptible to getting a sinus or ear infection due to the air quality in California. The doctor might prescribe an antibiotic to take with you.

Edna always has at least one month's worth of all Lauren's supplies and medicine at home. She suggests that if you will be traveling near the end of your supplies, you order early. This will avoid having to ask the trusted neighbor or friend to send you supplies.

If you are taking an electric wheelchair or scooter, have your equipment dealer check the batteries and make sure they are the gel type that is required by the airlines.

If you or your child has a serious medical condition, Medic Alert˚ has bracelets, necklaces and wallet cards that you can carry with you. Your emergency medical information and an emergency number where more complex information is stored are available in case you are unable to provide it yourself http://www.medicalert.org.

If you have a child who is prone to wander, My Precious Kid at http://www.mypreciouskid.com/ has shoe tags and also temporary tattoos that you can use with a marker to list your phone number. They also have a clip-on teddy bear (plastic) that emits a 86-db sound when activated by a key chain the parent carries, should a child wander away. They have a number of practical kid products and a special needs section as well.

Begin reading Disney stories or watching those Disney movies with your kids so they can relate to the rides and characters they will see there. If you have a child with autism or sensory integration issues, start talking to your child about Disneyland˚ Resort early. Show photos of the rides. Print the "Picture Communication Board" from our blog and familiarize yourself and your child with it. Almost everything about Disneyland˚ Resort is overly stimulating. If your child has "coping strategies," reinforce them. If he uses weighted blankets, weighted vests, other vests or clothing that gives more grounding, has toys or other things that are comforting, take them and use them. More discussion of this will follow in chapter 9. We have included links to YouTube videos of each ride at Disneyland˚ Resort. Viewing these may help prepare some children.

Even if you or your child is ambulatory at home, if you have a physical disability or weakness you may want to take your own wheelchair or rent one for use at Disneyland˚ Resort and Disney's California Adventure˚ Park. It is estimated that visitors walk up to six miles or more each day in the parks. If you rent a wheelchair at Disneyland˚ Park and then want to go to Disney's California Adventure˙ Park you can use that same wheelchair; same for renting a wheelchair inside Disney's California Adventure˙ Park. If you wish to go to Downtown Disney˙ District, however, you cannot take the wheelchair.

Transporter chairs are a nice option. They typically weigh 15-17 pounds and cost between $99-200. Sue purchased one a few years ago for Dustin because he not only tires, but wanders from activities that are overly stimulating. These chairs have small wheels and cannot be wheeled by the occupant.

(Sue's note: We are part of an online support group for children and adults with limb differences. If you or your child has a prosthesis, orthotics or other medical equipment, you might wish to print out TSA's guidelines and take a copy with you, should you encounter any problems.) http://www.tsa.gov/travelers/airtravel/specialneeds/index.shtm

CHAPTER 2

Packing & Getting Ready to Leave Your House, Pets, Plants, etc.

Welcome to an organized plan to make your stay at Disneyland® Resort less stressful. "Well organized Edna" is the one to thank for most of the information here. "Lackadaisical Sue" benefited greatly from the ideas and lists from Edna.

LIST #1–ITEMS YOU COULD SHIP AHEAD TO YOUR HOTEL

This is a rather exhaustive list that you can taper from or add to for your own needs. We tried to think of everything our own kids could possibly need. (Sue's comment: I would not have thought of shipping items ahead had Edna not suggested the idea. Edna always ships items to the hotel. It saved us hauling a lot of heavy cans of nutritional supplies through the airport. The sheer bulk and weight of needed items would have added to the cost of the airplane flight. We also sent snacks and microwavable pasta dishes.)

Ask the hotel what you need to write on the outside of the boxes. On the outside of each box Edna writes her name, date of arrival and confirmation number, and 1 of 1, 1 of 3, etc. Inside each box write on a large piece of paper your name, cell phone number, your date of arrival, hotel name and address and phone number—in case a box gets mangled up somehow and they need to open it up to see if there is ID inside.

List #1

- [ ] Diapers, diaper doublers, swim diapers, pull-ups
- [ ] Urinary supplies, as necessary
- [ ] Disposable underpads
- [ ] Small washable underpad to put on wheelchair seat in case of accidents
- [ ] Baby wipes/wet wipes; disinfectant wipes if you need them
- [ ] Gauze 4x4s/ 2x2s/ IV gauze
- [ ] Extra gastrostomy tubes/gastrostomy buttons; syringes as needed
- [ ] Tubing for gastrostomy button
- [ ] Tubing and yaunkers for suction machine
- [ ] Vinegar, if there is no store nearby, for cleaning suction machine
- [ ] Misting bottles to keep you cool in California
- [ ] Denture cleaner tablets for cleaning bottles or dentures
- [ ] Pipe cleaners for cleaning straw-cups or straw/bottles
- [ ] Extra straw cups and straw-tubing
- [ ] Large trash bags for diapers, etc (trash cans in hotel rooms are small and some hotels do not use trash can liners)
- [ ] Aluminum foil or plastic bags for yucky diapers; gloves
- [ ] Kleenex–purse size packs
- [ ] Hand sanitizer; disinfectant soaps, if you use
- [ ] Nail clippers; tweezers; scissors; cotton swabs
- [ ] Anti-diarrhea medicine; anti-gas product if needed
- [ ] Shower cap or whatever you use to keep water out of child's eyes during hair washing
- [ ] Blow dryer and/or iron, if hotel doesn't have and you need one (Sue rarely irons, Edna does need one)
- [ ] Quarters for hotel laundry

- [ ] Pre-measured laundry soap and dryer sheets, in sealed bags
- [ ] Laundry bag
- [ ] Timer (if needed for giving medicine) or set your cell phone alarms
- [ ] Pill crusher
- [ ] Razor (electric or other) & the charger
- [ ] Extra watch if you still wear one
- [ ] Feminine hygiene items
- [ ] Pre-addressed and stamped postcards, or addresses and stamps
- [ ] Lotions, skin remedies, sunscreen (a must)
- [ ] Mouth/gum pain medicine if child is teething
- [ ] Small bottles to put one day's medicine in for taking to the park during the day
- [ ] Small blankets to keep legs warm, especially in the evening
- [ ] If your digestive medicines come in large, bulky container, take some out for carry on and send the remainder ahead. (Our cardinal rule is to always hand-carry all medication, but some containers are too bulky.)
- [ ] Suppositories, enemas, if needed
- [ ] Snacks
- [ ] Nutritional formulas
- [ ] Disposable bowls, plates, silverware for use in hotel
- [ ] Pizza cutter for cutting food into smaller pieces; can opener
- [ ] Knife for cutting up fruit—you cannot take sharp objects into the parks but a sharp knife can be used in hotel room
- [ ] Needle, thread, safety pins
- [ ] Band-Aids® and other first aid supplies, like Neosporin® type ointments
- [ ] Wide (strapping) tape to use on the box to ship souvenirs or unused items home

☐ Tape for taping notes for maids to mirror in hotel room. (For those who are sensitive to odors or chemicals, there is a sign in English/Spanish at the end of the Resources section that you may post in your hotel room to ask that no sprays be used.)

☐ Heavy string, rope or plastic zip ties (Edna had the experience of being away from home when Lauren's tilt-in-space wheelchair mechanism broke. She used heavy string she had in the car to hold the chair upright.)

☐ Zip style bags for taking snacks to the park during the day

☐ Rain gear

☐ Umbrella (Edna uses an umbrella that clips to a wheelchair/stroller to keep the sun off Lauren)

☐ Autograph book and fat pen if you want to obtain character autographs

☐ Heating pad, ice packs

Any other medical supplies you require

☐ The Neat Sheet°, a lightweight, compact, water- and sand-proof sheet for sitting on the ground. Made by Kimberly Clark; readily available online or at local stores.

If you plan to be at the park after dark, flashing lights like bike riders use will help people see wheelchair users in the crowds; place these on the front of the wheelchair.

LIST #2–PRE-PACKING EACH DAY'S SUPPLIES & SHIPPING THEM AHEAD

Edna sends pre-packed items for each day at Disneyland° Resort in a see-through plastic bag. She labels the bags by date and day of the week. Each night she grabs the next day's supplies and puts it into Lauren's backpack. This way she doesn't need to figure out each night what supplies she needs for the following day. Although she doesn't UPS money to the hotel, once there she places a certain amount of money into only the next day's plastic bag, so she knows how much she will spend that day. The remainder of the money is placed in the room safe. This is what Edna includes in her daily bags. Your items may be different depending on your needs.

List #2

- ☐ The amount of diapers needed for one day
- ☐ Extra clothes and bibs expected for a day's use
- ☐ Hand towels and washcloths. Edna cuts small disposable under pads in half to use while giving Lauren drinks.
- ☐ Baby wipes or other wet wipes
- ☐ Extra syringes for liquid medicine
- ☐ Plastic bag or two for wet items
- ☐ Snack items and liquids
- ☐ Edna keeps medicine in the room safe and each night puts the next day's supply, plus a bit more, into the bag or backpack

LIST #3–ITEMS TO TAKE ON THE PLANE AS CARRY-ON

Pack in your carry-on anything that you cannot live without in case your luggage is lost or delayed (glasses, prescription meds etc). Pack all your valuables in your carry-on.

List #3

NOTE: MEDICATION. *Never under any circumstances place medication in checked luggage. Take it as carry-on.* It is not the fault of the airline if your medicine is unavailable if you need it before or on the flight, during layovers, delayed flights or if your luggage gets lost.

- ☐ Medication taken on daily/weekly basis. Liquids must be placed in clear zipper style bags for inspection by security. Although the phrase "quart size zip lock bag" is used, you may use gallon size bags if your liquid medication does not fit into a quart size bag.

☐ Keep all medications in zipper-style bags together so the security people can view it all at once and not have to dump the contents of your carry-on to see the medication. Again, you may use gallon size if your medication does not all fit into a quart size bag.

☐ Airline tickets; AAA card; keys

☐ Shuttle service phone number/confirmation number of shuttles in case plane is delayed

☐ Hotel name, phone number/confirmation number in case plane is delayed

☐ Disneyland® Resort personal assistance phone number: 714-781-7290. The people at this phone number can answer just about any questions you have.

☐ Passport, drivers license (or state ID for non-drivers); airlines require photo identification for all adult passengers

☐ Birth certificate for child under age two

☐ Proof of automobile insurance if renting a car

☐ Medical card or insurance papers

☐ Parking permit for the disabled

☐ Notes from doctor, if needed

☐ Guardianship papers, if necessary

☐ Booklet listing all of disabled and other family members' information (diagnoses, allergies and the like, doctors, medications, emergency contacts)

☐ All money, in all forms

☐ The numbers on your travelers checks in case they are lost or stolen (pack separately from traveler's checks)

☐ Dollar bills for tipping

- [ ] Any pre-purchased Disney tickets

- [ ] Lip balm (you must place this in a zip-lock type bag for security inspection by TSA)

- [ ] Extra eye glasses and/or contact lenses; sunglasses

- [ ] Contact lens solution (no more than 3 ounces) must be placed in a clear zipper style bag for inspection by TSA

- [ ] Medication for nausea and pain; asthma rescue inhaler

- [ ] Deodorant; sunscreen

- [ ] Syringes and supplies for giving medicine on the plane (Clamp for g-tube/g-button; gauze; tubing for g-button; gloves; timer for medicine)

- [ ] Tube feeding and supplies if needed on plane

- [ ] Wheelchair tools less than seven inches in length may be carried on.

- [ ] Cell phone and charger

- [ ] Extra diapers and extra clothing; bibs

- [ ] Suction machine or other sensitive medical equipment that should not go as cargo—feeding pump, etc.

- [ ] Misting bottle to mist warm child if needed

- [ ] Snacks

- [ ] Liquids to drink (only liquids that have been purchased after you have gone through security will be allowed unless it is canned nutritional formula; even so, Sue was questioned about canned formula)

- [ ] Baby bottles, straw drinking bottles or special cups for a person with a disability

- [ ] Baby wipes/wet wipes

- [ ] Hand towels or paper towels

- [ ] Plastic bag for wet bibs, etc.

- [ ] Lightweight blanket for legs, if needed

☐ Sweater, jacket, shawl

☐ Pad and pen if taking notes about trip

☐ Video camera; still camera

☐ Lanyard, fanny pack, visor, hat

LIST #4–PACKING YOUR CHECKED LUGGAGE

In each piece of luggage, including carry-on, write your name, address, cell phone number, hotel, and hotel phone number, in case bags get lost or tags get torn off somehow. *We repeat: under no circumstances ever place medication in checked luggage.*

List #4

☐ Pants, long and short; capris, jeans

☐ Shirts/tops: long and short sleeve, sleeveless/tank tops; T-shirts; blouses

☐ Nightclothes: pajamas, nighties, boxers

☐ Underwear: undershirts, underpants, bras, socks

☐ Outer wear: sweater, shawl, jacket, sweatshirt, coat, rain poncho (useful on wet rides on cool days)

☐ Footwear (wear comfortable shoes that are already broken-in), shoes, flip-flops, slippers

☐ Swimwear: swimsuits/trunks, goggles, personal floatation devices, if necessary

☐ All chargers for medical equipment except cell phone charger which you take as carry-on

☐ Curling iron and hair dryer (if hotel doesn't offer these)

☐ Sharp knife or scissors for cutting tape on the boxes you ship to your hotel

GETTING YOUR HOME, PETS AND PLANTS READY FOR YOUR TRIP

Stop your mail and newspaper or arrange for a trusted neighbor or friend to pick them up daily. Arrange for indoor and outdoor plants to be watered and for watering of a garden if needed. Arrange for pets to be fed and watered or take them to a kennel. If you will be gone for more than one week, check refrigerator for anything that is getting old and could spoil and leave a bad odor.

Have your neighbor check your house for deliveries so things do not sit out – medical supplies that might be on automatic delivery and supplies that are ordered month by month need to be inside.

Edna turns off the water to the washing machine and toilet and unplugs things like the microwave oven, freestanding stove, dryer, lamps, toaster, etc. If you have a big job like cleaning the outdoor hot tub that will need to be done soon, try to do that prior to leaving so you can come home and not have the job facing you.

If driving, have car serviced—you don't want to have an emergency on the way such as air conditioning going out.

If you are traveling when you may have flood weather at home, and you routinely use an automatic sump pump, be sure to turn it on. Let a neighbor know you will be gone and give your itinerary and phone number to them in case there is an emergency at home—leave a key to your house with the neighbor, too. (Sue left the trusted friend a key, and while they were gone the trusted friend locked herself out of the house and the neighbor had to break in. Sue should have had this part of the list before she left.)

Be certain to lock all windows and doors and put alarm system on. Show a neighbor where and how to turn your system off if it does alarm. Mow the lawn so your home has that "lived in" look. If you will be absent for awhile, make arrangements for someone to keep the grass short and watered so it appears that someone is home.

Home improvement and hardware stores have timers that are easy to set for lights and/or radio inside your house. This also gives the appearance of someone being home. Another lighting technique that is easy to do is purchasing and installing a motion detector for your outdoor lights. (Sue left flowers for her neighbor before a trip and set off their motion detector light at about 4 AM – how embarrassing!)

CHAPTER 3
Flying to Disneyland® Resort

IN THE WEEKS BEFORE YOU LEAVE

Check with friends for rides to and from the airport. Check your local phone directory for shuttle services that will take you to and from the airport. Make sure the vehicle can take a wheelchair. A friend can also drive your own vehicle and drop you off and pick you up from the airport. (This option worked for Sue and her family. Her friend then parked their vehicle in the driveway while they were away.)

If you park your car at the airport, plan to park in an economy lot or a park and ride lot. Phone the airport to see what is available and how expensive it might be. If you are driving to an airport that is some distance from your home, many motels and hotels near major airports offer parking at reduced rates for patrons while they are gone.

Take a cab (may require reserving ahead to get an accessible vehicle).

48 HOURS BEFORE YOU LEAVE

Phone your airline or check online to confirm your reservations.

WITHIN 24 HOURS BEFORE YOU LEAVE

Within 24 hours before your flight is scheduled to leave, you may (as of this writing) print your boarding passes. This does save time, especially if you use curbside checking. Once at the airport, you simply go through security and go to your flight gate.

USING CURBSIDE CHECK-IN

If your airline has curbside check-in, this is definitely a plus. Sue used United's curbside check-in for $2.00 per bag. The attendant must see photo identification for each adult traveling in the party. All bags must have a tag. For United, each bag had to weigh less than 50 pounds or there were additional charges. The nice thing about using curbside check-in and already having the boarding passes printed was not having to wait in any lines at the airline counter, but just be able to proceed directly to security and the boarding gate.

SECURITY

The Transportation Security Administration or TSA has a toll free number at 866-289-9673. You can call them or go to their website at http://www.tsa.gov/travelers/airtravel/specialneeds/index.shtm for questions you may have about security checks for people with disabilities and about guidelines and rules for carry-on items. They are easy to reach at their toll free number and are available 24 hours a day.

(Sue's note: My three children who are wheelchair users did not encounter any problems with security. The agents checked the chairs thoroughly. Our "problems" were with carry-on items. I did not realize that lip balm-type items needed to be in a zip-lock bag. I was questioned about a set of Allen wrenches for Carl's wheelchair—it seems to need frequent repairs—and I was asked about a can of feeding formula. On the return trip, I inadvertently left a bottle of chocolate milk in a carry-on that I was questioned about. They did not, however, bat an eye over Carl's Epi-Pen injection for his latex allergy. Isabel did not have any problems with her scooter.) (Edna's note: Lauren and I have never had any problems with security.)

BOARDING

Make certain you let an airline attendant know you will need to board early and/or if you need an aisle chair. They will also need to tag any wheelchair or scooter that will be put under the plane.

Edna reminded Sue that airlines used to require tagging any part of a wheelchair that could come off. They do not go to the trouble now, but if a part is detachable, it would be safest to stick an address label in an out of the way place, just in case. (Sue lost one of the "side guards" on Carl's chair on her recent trip. She did not label detachable parts.)

Airlines allow a person using a wheelchair to wheel to the airplane door and transfer to an aisle chair, if necessary. The chair or scooter is then taken and loaded under the plane with the cargo and luggage.

ON THE FLIGHT

During the flight, it is rare to be served a meal without ordering it ahead, and then it is usually a sandwich. Most folks who need to have a meal will need to bring something with them or purchase a meal in the airport before boarding. Remember that you CANNOT bring beverages through the security area. Beverages are usually served on flights and there may be cookies, crackers or pretzels.

GETTING OFF THE PLANE

Generally, anyone requiring assistance or waiting for their wheelchair or scooter to be brought to the door, will be the last off the plane. You can ask for extra assistance. When Sue and her crew arrived at LAX, two of United Airline's staff volunteered to accompany them to the baggage area and load their baggage onto a Smart Cart (luggage carts that can be rented for around $3.00 with quarters or a debit/credit card). Smart Carts are worth the price if you have a good bit of luggage and limited luggage carriers.

SOCIAL STORY ABOUT GOING ON A PLANE TRIP

Story by Johanna Frohm with permission of the author

Going on a   plane   trip.

At the   airport,   listen   and   watch.

Show   your   plane ticket   and   picture ID.

Put   your   shoes   and   suitcase   on   the   conveyor belt.

Walk through the scanner.   A guard may check your bag.

A guard may use a wand to check your clothes.   Walk to your plane.

Enjoy   your   trip.

The Picture Communication Symbols ©1981–2010 by DynaVox Mayer-Johnson LLC. All Rights Reserved Worldwide. Used with permission.

SOCIAL STORY ABOUT GOING THROUGH SECURITY

Story by Johanna Frohm with permission of the author

Going on a   plane   trip

show photo identification and plane ticket

place shoes in bin and bag on belt

walk through scanner

guard may search bag

guard may check with wand

walk to plane

The Picture Communication Symbols ©1981–2010 by DynaVox Mayer-Johnson LLC. All Rights Reserved Worldwide. Used with permission.

CHAPTER 4

Getting From the Airport to Your Hotel

HOTEL TRANSPORTATION

Be sure that the hotel transportation has wheelchair access, if you need it.

TAXI

Taxis are expensive, about $85 from Los Angeles/LAX to Anaheim, $45 from Orange County/SNA and about $50 from Long Beach/LGB.

SUPERSHUTTLE

The Supershuttle at 800 BLUEVAN (800-258-3826) www.supershuttle.com provides transportation from the airports for $16 per person from LAX and lesser amounts from the other two airports nearby. Supershuttle is open 24 hours a day for reservations AND they are open 24 hours a day to shuttle folks to their destinations. If you need a wheelchair van with a lift, they have several such vans. When making a reservation, let them know you will need an accessible van. They like to have 24-48 hours notice, but seem able to accommodate people with somewhat less notice. The price is the same for regular and wheelchair vans. Edna and Lauren always use Supershuttle and love it.

DISNEYLAND® RESORT EXPRESS

Disneyland˙ Resort Express runs buses from the airports to Anaheim. They can be reached at 714-978-8855 or 800-828-6699. http://www.graylineanaheim.com/airport_info.shtml. Wheelchair accessible coaches available upon request.

RENTAL CARS & ACCESSIBLE RENTAL VANS

Rental cars and accessible vans are available near the airports from the nationwide and local car rental agencies. Hertz referred Sue to three companies that rent accessible vans. Of the three, two had no vans available during our stay. She phoned the week before. The one company that told her they had a van did not have it available the day they arrived, and further phone tag proved fruitless. (Sue's suggestion: get something in writing way ahead of time.) The three choices follow:

- Accessible Vans of America http://www.mobilityworks.com; 800-687-4446 or 818-780-1788

- Wheelers http://www.wheelersvanrentals.com/LosAngeles/ CA Toll-Free 1-866-859-8880

- Wheelchair Getaways www.wheelchairgetaways.com; 800-659-1972

AS YOU PASS THROUGH YOUR HOTEL/MOTEL LOBBY...

While in your hotel, check the racks of offers available in the Anaheim and LA area. There are often specials for tours of the area and coupons with discounts for meals at local restaurants.

Each month, the *Visitors Entertainment Guide* has a monthly calendar for Disneyland˙ Park and Disney's California Adventure˙ Park that list the opening and closing times for each park and include a short list of the daily activities. The *Visitors Entertainment Guide* also includes tours with special rates, restaurant specials (many include their menus and prices), the local TV guide and best maps of local surface streets.

The *Visitors Entertainment Guide* is available at 154 local hotels and business establishments or online at http://www.visguideoc.com/. They can be reached at 714-633-0355 for questions.

CHAPTER 5

Getting from your hotel to Disneyland® Resort

WALK

If you are staying close to the East Shuttle parking area or at Disneyland˙ Resort, it is only a short walk.

ANAHEIM RESORT TRANSIT

(ART) www.rideart.org, 888-364 2787

ART is a transportation system used by many, many hotels in the Anaheim Resort area. The buses and trolleys stop at many of the hotels and provide transportation to Disneyland˙ Resort. ART buses do not stop at each and every hotel/motel. Hotels that are close together share one stop. For instance, Edna and Lauren stayed at the Ramada Limited Suites, and the three other hotels adjacent to the Ramada used Ramada's bus stop. At press time, there are 16 routes. All the ART buses have wheelchair lifts. Folks in wheelchairs are loaded first.

The buses make a run approximately every 20 minutes. The buses begin running one hour before Disneyland˙ Resort opens and continue half an hour after Disneyland˙ Resort closes. Each hotel will have ART operating hours and the Disneyland˙ Resort operating hours so you can make plans.

There are three ways to purchase full day ART passes. Multiple day passes are also available.

- On the Internet and have them waiting at your hotel www.rideart.org
- Hotels that the ART serves sell tickets
- At ART kiosk locations

If for some reason you neglect to get a full day pass, you can pay exact cash for a one-way fare. Drivers do not sell passes. Full day passes can be used as often as you like on the day the pass is good.

The ART buses have their own loading/unloading area at Disneyland® Resort. Each route is numbered and signs designate where each route loads and unloads. It is a pretty foolproof system. Edna had no problems so it must be easy. If you leave something on an ART bus, call their lost and found at 714-507-1111.

At press time ART fares are: **Adult:** One-Way cash $3; All day pass for one day $4; Three day pass $10; Five day pass $16. **Child ages 3-9:** One-way cash $1; All day pass for one day $1; Three day pass $2; Five day pass $4. **Children age 2 and under ride free.**

HOTEL TRANSPORTATION

If you need accessible transportation from your hotel, ask if the hotel provides that service. Many hotels are served by ART.

TAXI CAB AND BUS

Yellow Cab serving Anaheim can be reached at 800-535-2211.

Orange County Transportation Authority (OCTA). 714-560-5932. OCTA is the public bus transportation serving Anaheim. Visit http://www.octa.net/ for schedules and routes.

YOUR OWN CAR OR RENTAL

You can drive your own car or a rental. Parking is available at the Disney lots for $11/day and up for larger vehicles. You can leave and return in the same day at no extra charge. Trams to the entrance plaza with ramp service for wheelchair users are available from the Timon parking lot and from the Mickey and Friends parking structure. To see what the parking trams are like, check out YouTube http://www.youtube.com/watch?v=eilkdZZrXXo.

CHAPTER 6

Overview of Disneyland® Resort

ENTERING DISNEYLAND® RESORT AND DISNEY'S CALIFORNIA ADVENTURE® PARK

As you enter from either tram, the ART or walking and are headed toward the plaza, you will pass through a security area, with tables where Disney Cast Members check all bags as guests enter the park. (Sue asked what they were checking for and was told dangerous items, weapons, glass containers or "excessive amounts of food.") This should take only a few minutes. It is not like TSA at the airports but is simply a visual inspection of bags and backpacks.

BUYING ADMISSION TICKETS

After exiting the security area you will enter the plaza between Disney's California Adventure Park® and Disneyland® Park. There are ticket booths in the plaza where you can purchase admission tickets. There are tickets for each park, Park Hopper® tickets (that allow you to go to both parks in a given day), multiple day admissions and annual passes. The lines can be lengthy depending on how busy the park is that day. Most hotels in the area also sell tickets if you have not purchased the tickets ahead.

If you have pre-purchased tickets or have online barcode tickets you may proceed to the entrance through turnstiles. Bar code "tickets" will be exchanged for regular tickets there. Each set of turnstiles has a gate for wheelchair users and those with strollers.

DISNEYLAND® PARK AND DISNEY'S CALIFORNIA ADVENTURE® PARK MAPS

At the entrance you will be given a map of the park. Each park has its own colorful map with drawings of the rides. Take enough for each person in your party. The maps are full of useful information about the park. The legend has symbols to help you find restrooms, first aid, information areas, phones, ATMs and a host of other places. There is printed information about FASTPASS® and PhotoPass®. These maps also have a picture code next to each ride that will tell you about mobility accommodations and accommodations for the hearing impaired.

There is a symbol indicating that an attraction may be frightening for children and another that indicates that the attraction has physical considerations. "Physical considerations" are Disney's warnings about the rides. For safety on active rides they advise being in good health, free from high blood pressure, free from heart, back and neck problems, not prone to motion sickness and using caution of you have a condition that could be worsened by the ride. Expectant mothers are advised not to ride some attractions.

DISNEY *ENTERTAINMENT TIMES GUIDE*

Also pick up a Disney *Entertainment Times Guide.* Disneyland® Park is on one side of the Entertainment Guide and Disney's California Adventure® Park is on the other side. These guides have the current dates they are valid for listed at the very top of the brochure. The guide lists:

Shows and Parades including times and routes. Times for fireworks and Fantasmic! are here. Also listed are the times that certain attractions or areas of the park may close earlier than the rest of the park. Remember, if you have Park Hopper® tickets, that Disneyland® Park and Disney's California Adventure® Park often have separate hours of operation.

Shows and Live Music lists other shows and live music and the places and times for such.

Disney Characters lists the times that Disney characters will make special appearances in the parks. Check the *Entertainment Times Guide* for information on locations and times. Edna reminds you that Cast Members guide the characters and will monitor the lines to view characters. Characters do not stay "forever" and Cast Members guide guests to the characters in an orderly fashion. A Cast Member monitors the "end" of the line and will inform you if no more guests can be accommodated. Besides these character times, characters are often out and

Lauren & Beauty and the Beast

about unannounced, especially if there are large crowds waiting for events to begin. Characters will pose with any guests and often Cast Members will snap a photo on your camera or a willing guest will take a photo for you. At some places in the parks, Disney photographers will snap photos on their cameras and give you a PhotoPass˚. FASTPASS˚ attractions are also listed in the Entertainment Guide.

PARADES

Both Disneyland˚ Park and Disney's California Adventure˚ Park offer parades. Check the *Entertainment Times Guide* under Shows and Parades for daily times. Parade routes are on the Disneyland˚ Park and Disney's California Adventure˚ Park maps. In Disneyland˚ Park there are special areas set aside for wheelchair users to view the parade. It is always good to be at the parade route well ahead of time. If you have questions about wheelchair viewing areas, ask a Cast Member or check in with Guest Services/Relations.

LOST CHILDREN

If your child becomes lost, he/she will be taken to "Lost Children" which is next to First Aid in Disneyland˚ Park and is next to the Baby Care Center in Disney's California Adventure˚ Park.

RESTAURANTS AND FOOD CARTS

Disneyland® Park, Disney's California Adventure® Park and Downtown Disney® District offer a wide selection in dining. Disney restaurant menu selections change often therefore Braille menus and large print menus are not available. Sue was told by a manager at Guest Relations that any Cast Member would "happily read the menu" to any guest who requires that assistance. For information about restaurants and their menu selections and prices please check this website: http://www.themouseforless.com/tripplanning/menus/dl/menus.shtml

Food carts in Disneyland® Park and Disney's California Adventure® Park offer apples, oranges, pineapple spears, grapes and slices of watermelon. If you need to cut the fruit, many of the carts have plastic knives and forks. Soda pop, vitamin water and bottled water are also available. Cast Members sell popcorn, churros and ice cream at carts scattered around the parks.

GUEST SERVICES/GUEST RELATIONS

Now, before everyone runs off to play, make sure you visit Guest Services. In Disneyland® Park, it is located in City Hall. This is to the left of the Main Street Train Station as you enter, or ask any Cast Member. In Disney's California Adventure® Park, the Guest Relations Lobby is to the left of the turnstiles as you enter.

Special Needs Passes

Guest Services/Relations will help you get the most out of your visit if you are traveling with someone who has a disability. When Sue spoke with Guest Services, they said they will write Special Needs Passes to meet each person's individual needs. This is more likely if an individual's disability is not apparent from outward appearances. Sue asked if one needed to bring some "proof" of their condition and was told that was not necessary, but you should have the person with you who needs the pass, and explain the needs that you would like addressed. Perhaps you are traveling with someone with sensory regulation issues or autism. You explain your needs and the pass is written with you in mind.

Extensive information for parents of children with autism or sensory integration issues is found in Chapter 9.

Special Needs Brochures

Disney has six separate color-coded guides for folks with special needs that explain applicable accommodations for the attractions. Pick these up at the Guest Relations Lobby at Disney's California Adventure® Park or at Guest Services at the City Hall in Disneyland® Park. (Similar information is also online. For downloads in a pdf format, see the following link: http://disneyland.disney.go.com/plan/guest-services/guests-with-disabilities/)

Attraction Access for Guests Using Wheelchairs and Electric Convenience Vehicles (ECVs) (light yellow brochure)

This brochure lists attractions and their adjustments for visitors with mobility impairments. Roughly half the attractions require a person with a physical disability to leave the wheelchair to experience the attraction. Some rides have special vehicles that allow you to remain in your wheelchair. Still other attractions have transfer accessible vehicles if you are able to transfer from your wheelchair across to the seat of the attraction (see photo of Dumbo ride in Chapter 7). Other attractions require the ability to walk for varying distances and some require the ability to climb up or down to access the ride vehicle. There are some attractions that require transferring from an ECV to a manual wheelchair available at the attraction. Cast Members are not allowed to assist guests on and off ride vehicles. Members of your family or party may help you. In Chapters 7 and 8 there are details about each ride.

Many attractions require entering through the exit for accessibility. These "auxiliary" entrances are not for the purpose of bypassing waiting in line. (Sue's note: we were in the auxiliary entrance for Pirates of the Caribbean and were told the wait would be up to an hour since only six groups with a person with a physical disability could be accommodated in the ride at one time. So, just to let you know, the wait could at times be longer than the wait time through the regular entrance.) For a listing of rides by their mobility requirements, go to:

http://adisneyland.disney.go.com/media/dlr_v0200/en_US/help/Mobility_201009.pdf

You may remain in your wheelchair to experience the following attractions at Disneyland® Park:

- Jungle Cruise
- Enchanted Tiki Room
- The Many Adventures of Winnie the Pooh
- Disney Princess Fantasy Faire
- King Arthur Carrousel
- Sleeping Beauty Castle Walkthrough (accessible experience only)
- Big Thunder Ranch
- Fantasmic!
- Frontierland Shootin' Exposition
- The Golden Horseshoe Stage
- Mark Twain Riverboat
- Pirate's Lair on Tom Sawyer Island
- The Disneyland® Story featuring Great Moments with Mr. Lincoln
- Main Street Cinema
- Disneyland® Railroad (except Main Street Station)
- Goofy's Playhouse
- Mickey's House and Meet Mickey
- Minnie's House
- Marine Observation Outpost (MOO) at *Finding Nemo* Submarine Voyage
- Disneyland® Monorail
- Captain EO starring Michael Jackson
- Innoventions

- Starcade
- Buzz Light Year Astro Blasters

For attractions in Disney's California Adventure˚ Park, folks with mobility impairments enter attractions through the regular lines. The following attractions in Disney's California Adventure˚ Park may be accessed in your wheelchair:

- Bountiful Valley Farm
- It's Tough to be a Bug
- Flik's Fun Fair
- Princess Dot Puddle Park
- The Bakery Tour, hosted by Boudin˚ Foods
- Mission Tortilla Factory, hosted by Mission˚ Foods
- Redwood Creek Challenge Trail (accessible routes only)
- Disney Animation
- Hyperion Theater
- Monsters Inc. Mike and Sully to the Rescue!
- Muppet*Vision 3D
- Playhouse Disney - Live on Stage
- Midway Games of the Boardwalk
- King Trion's Carousel
- SS Rustworthy
- Mickey's Fun Wheel
- Toy Story Midway Mania!

Information on Services for Guests with Visual Disabilities (green brochure)

Three types of accommodations are available for guests with visual impairments: Braille Guidebooks, Audio Description and Digital Audio Tours.

Braille Guidebooks:

To borrow a Disneyland˚ Park Braille Guidebook requires a $20 refundable deposit. The book is available at Guest Services in City Hall. The book *must* be returned on the same day it is borrowed. Phone ahead to (714) 781-7290 to check availability of Disney California Adventure˚ Park Braille Guidebooks.

Audio Description:

Audio Description provides descriptions of some visual elements of the attraction such as actions, descriptions of settings and scene changes. To take advantage of this service one must borrow A Disney Handheld Device. A $25 refundable deposit is required. The device must be returned on the same day. One wears this device at chest level (you can wear headphones or a wireless device in your ear). When you are near attractions with this feature, the device will automatically be activated. The device goes into a "sleep" mode after you leave the attraction. Audio Description is available at the following attractions in Disneyland˚ Park:

- Alice in Wonderland
- Buzz Lightyear Astro Blasters
- Disneyland˚ Railraod
- Enchanted Tiki Room
- *Finding Nemo* Submarine Voyage
- Haunted Mansion
- Captain EO
- "it's a small world"
- Mr. Toad's Wild Ride
- Peter Pan's Flight
- Pinocchio's Daring Journey
- Pirates of the Caribbean

- Snow White's Scary Adventure
- Storybook Land Canal Boats
- The Many Adventures of Winnie the Pooh

At Disney California Adventure Park:

- It's Tough to be a Bug!
- Monsters Inc. Mike & Sulley to the Rescue!
- Muppet*Vision 3D
- Disney Animation–Turtle Talk with Crush

Digital Audio Tours:

Digital Audio Tours are available for each park at Guest Services/Relations. A Digital Audio Tour gives the guest a brief description of guest services and attractions. The digital audio devices are available for a $25 refundable deposit (refundable when returned on the same day). There are a limited number of these devices available on a first-come, first-served basis. For a listing of attractions by their visual disability accommodations, go to: http://adisneyland. disney.go.com/media/dlr_v0200/en_US/help/VisualDisability_201009.pdf

Information on Services for Guests with Service Animals (yellow brochure)

Disneyland® Resort allows service animals into the parks, but they must remain on a leash or harness at all times. This brochure states that guests with service animals must access the attractions through the standard queue. You may inquire at City Hall or Guest Relations Lobby to find out what is necessary if you have both a mobility impairment and a service dog.

Service animals are not allowed on these attractions:

In Disneyland⁻ Park:

- Star Tours
- Space Mountain
- Gadget's Go Coaster, presented by Sparkle˙
- Goofy's Playhouse
- Indiana Jones˜ Adventure
- Big Thunder Mountain Railroad
- Splash Mountain
- Matterhorn Bobsleds

In Disney's California Adventure⁻ Park:

- Tuck and Roll's Drive'Em Buggies
- Grizzly River Run
- Soarin' Over California
- The Twilight Zone Tower of Terror™
- Jumpin' Jellyfish
- Maliboomer
- Mulholland Madness, presented by Alamo
- Mickey's Fun Wheel
- California Screamin'

For a brochure detailing service animal regulations, go to http://adisneyland.disney.go.com/media/dlr_v0200/en_US/help/ServiceAnimal_201009.pdf

You are allowed to use open areas to relieve your service animal and then you are requested to contact a Cast Member for proper disposal. The Disneyland˙ Kennel is available for guests to use. In Disney Hotel areas, service animals must remain on their leash or harness unless they are in the guest's room.

Information on Services for Guests with Hearing Disabilities (orange brochure)

Disney offers seven types of accommodations, depending on the attraction, for individuals with hearing impairments. These are: telephone accommodations; sign language interpretation; reflective captioning; guest-activated captioning, also known as video captioning; written aids; assistive listening; and handheld captioning. A copy of the handout for guests with hearing disabilities is available online at this web address: http://adisneyland.disney.go.com/media/dlr_v0200/en_US/help/HearingDisability_201009.pdf

Telephones:

According to this brochure all telephones at Disneyland® Resort have amplification by pushing the # key or by a separate volume button on the phone. Pay phones with TTY (Text Typewriter) are available in Disneyland® Park at:

- Main Entry Plaza near Disneyland® Kennel Club
- In Disneyland® Park at Tomorrowland (near Space Mountain)

In Disney's California Adventure® Park:

- Golden State
- Hollywood Pictures Backlot (next to Hyperion Theater)
- Main Entrance (West Entry Plaza, next to restrooms)
- Paradise Pier (behind King Triton's Carousel)
- In Disneyland® Resort Hotels TTY phones are available upon request.

Assistive Listening Systems:

Assistive Listening amplifies sound and is recommended for people with mild to moderate hearing loss. The Disney Handheld Device is available for a $25 refundable deposit. This device not only amplifies sound at the specific attractions listed below, but also has Handheld Captioning for other specific attractions. Disney's Handheld Device may be used with headphones or with an induction loop and hands free earpiece (in one ear). The device is worn at chest height and automatically comes on to amplify the sound at these attractions:

<u>In Disneyland® Park:</u>

- Enchanted Tiki Room
- Captain EO starring Michael Jackson
- Innoventions (Honda exhibit only)
- Aladdin's Oasis (seasonal)

<u>In Disney's California Adventure® Park:</u>

- Disney Animation (Turtle Talk with Crush and Animation Academy)
- Hyperion Theater
- The Hollywood Backlot Stage
- It's Tough to be a Bug!
- Muppet*Vison 3D
- Playhouse Disney–Live on Stage!
- Redwood Creek Challenge Trail (Ahwahnee Camp Circle)

The device goes into a "sleep mode" when one is not in an area where the Assistive Listening functions.

Reflective Captioning:

Reflective Captioning is a new technology that uses a light-emitting diode (LED) to project the captions onto a panel in front of the user. Contact a Cast Member at the location to use this system.

It is available in Disneyland® Park at:

- Disneyland® Story featuring Great Moments with Mr. Lincoln
- Captain EO starring Michael Jackson

It is available in Disney's California Adventure® Park for the following attractions:

- It's Tough to be a Bug!
- Muppet*Vision 3D

Handheld Captioning:

Handheld captioning is available using Disney's Handheld Device available at Guest Relations/Services for a refundable $25 deposit. The device displays text at the following attractions:

At Disneyland® Park:

- Disneyland® Railroad (all stations)
- "it's a small world"
- Peter Pan's Flight
- Snow White's Scary Adventure
- Storybook Land Canal Boats
- Mr. Toad's Wild Ride
- Buzz Lightyear Astro Blasters
- Finding Nemo Submarine Voyage
- Enchanted Tiki Room
- Jungle Cruise
- Haunted Mansion
- Pirates of the Caribbean
- The Many Adventures of Winnie the Pooh

At Disney's California Adventure® Park:

- Monsters, Inc. Mike & Sulley to the Rescue!

Guest Activated Captioning, also known as Video Captioning:

There are caption ready monitors available at some attractions. The monitors are designated "CC." See a Cast Member who will activate the monitor.

In Disneyland® Park:

- Disneyland˚ Story featuring Great Moments with Mr. Lincoln
- Sleeping Beauty Castle Walkthrough (accessible experience only)
- Captain EO starring Michael Jackson
- Star Tours (preshow only)
- Space Mountain (preshow only)
- Marine Observation Outpost (MOO) at *Finding Nemo* Submarine Voyage
- Innoventions
- Indiana Jones˜ Adventure (preshow only)

In Disney's California Adventure˚ Park:

- Soarin' Over California (preshow only)
- Mission Tortilla Factory, hosted by Mission˚ Foods
- The Bakery Tour, hosted by Boudin˚ Foods
- Disney Animation (Courtyard/Lobby only)
- Muppet*Vision 3D
- Playhouse Disney–Live on Stage! (preshow only)
- The Twilight Zone Tower of Terror™ (preshow only)
- Toy Story Midway Mania!
- Walt Disney Imagineering Blue Sky Cellar

Written Aids:

There are packets of information for several attractions that include the dialogue and narration, a flashlight, pencil and paper. The brochure states that you can inquire about this prior to experiencing the attraction, and that a list of the attractions with written aids is available at City Hall or the Central Plaza in Disneyland® Park or at the Guest Relations Lobby in Disney's California Adventure® Park. It does explain that these items need to be immediately returned to the Cast Member following the show or attraction.

Sign Language Interpretation:

Beginning in June 2010 the Disneyland® Resort will provide Sign Language interpretation at specific shows on a rotating basis. In Disneyland® Park, Sign Language interpretation will be on Mondays and Saturdays, and at Disney's California Adventure® Park on Sundays and Fridays. If you would like to take advantage of this service, contact Guest Relations/Services at (714) 781-6167 (voice) or (714) 781-7292 (TTY) to request schedule of performances. You can also request sign language interpretation for other shows by calling (714) 781-6176 (voice) or (714) 781-7292 (TTY). Phone at least 7 days in advance.

Information on Show Lighting Effects (pink brochure)

This brochure mentions that Disney uses a wide variety of photo lighting effects throughout the parks on attractions and in many of the shows. Checking with your personal physician is recommended if you have photosensitivity or a seizure disorder. http://adisneyland.disney.go.com/media/dlr_v0200/en_US/help/Lighting_201009.pdf

Helpful Hints (blue brochure)

The Helpful Hints brochure offers suggestions to make your day at Disneyland® Resort more enjoyable by *Planning* and *Resting*.

Plan your day by consulting the Guide Maps and Entertainment Times Guide. The Information Board located in the Central Plaza on Main Street in Disneyland® Park and in Sunshine Plaza at Disney's California Adventure® Park provide show times as well as other up to the minute information on attraction wait times. Arriving 30-45 minutes ahead for shows and parades is recommended. As you plan, you may want to enjoy one area of the park before moving on to another to minimize the amount of walking you do, or you may want to utilize transportation attractions to move from one part of the park to another (such as the Disneyland® Railroad or Monorail). Remember to use Disney FASTPASS for popular attractions.

Rest by taking frequent breaks, sitting in the shade, sitting in an air-conditioned building, or taking in an attraction with a minimal wait time. Stay hydrated and use sunscreen. Both parks have First Aid if you need health assistance at any time. Packages may be checked at The Newsstand and Pioneer Mercantile in Disneyland® Park or at Engine-Ears at Disney's California Adventure® Park to lessen your load.

You may always ask any Cast Member for assistance. Their goal is to help you enjoy your day at Disneyland® Resort.

HELPFUL HINTS FOR THE ABLE-BODIED

The following are helpful hints from Edna for the able bodied so all will be safe traveling through the parks:

Watch out for wheelchair users. They are usually sitting at a lower level than you who walk. Be careful with those large purses, bags of souvenirs, other bags and backpacks. Slinging them around can hit small children and wheelchair users in the head. Remember that the squirming, kicking child you are holding has feet that are at the head height of most wheelchair users.

We know that cell phones are distracting to drivers; the same happens while walking. Be careful, especially in the dark when large crowds are leaving areas like Fantasmic! Try not to cut through lines in front of wheelchair users. A man who did this fell into the lap of Sue's son Carl.

Try not to stop suddenly or cross right in front of a wheelchair user or someone with a disability. (Sue drives a heavy van and always has to leave extra distance between her van and the car in front of her in order to have enough time and distance to stop her van. Wheelchair users and their caregivers have the same problem when someone stops suddenly in front of them. Wheelchair footrests are a real "killer" to the back of your legs.)

At parades, please don't stand in front of wheelchair users. Help restless children keep busy and make sure their new toy swords don't "stab" anyone. You might bring small bottles of bubbles or handheld game devices to occupy them.

In restrooms, please leave the large stalls open as wheelchairs do not fit into the small stalls. If you need the disability accommodations that Disney provides, be sure to utilize them; if you do not, then enjoy your day and leave them for those who need them.

If your kids ask, "What happened?" type questions, instead of "shushing" them, have them say "hi" to the person. This could be a conversation starter instead of an uncomfortable situation. Be nice. Smile. Everyone wants to have a great day at Disneyland˚ Resort!

FIRST AID STATIONS

Disneyland˚ Park and Disney's California Adventure˚ Park both have First Aid Stations. The one in Disneyland˚ Park is located near the Central Hub/Plaza on the right side of the street. The First Aid area in Disney's California Adventure˚ Park is located by the Tortilla Factory, behind the silos; ask if you do not see it. No matter where you are in the parks, if you have an emergency, contact the nearest Cast Member for assistance. Nurses are available at all times at the First Aid Stations.

Edna found out a lot about the First Aid Stations since Lauren needs to lie down daily for an hour or so. The First Aid Stations have cots in them and if you need to lie down, you may go there. Edna heard people asking for things she never dreamed were dispensed there: laxatives, antacids and medicine for upset stomach. They also dispense aspirin, acetaminophen, ibuprophen, Band-Aids˚, antiseptic, etc. All products are latex free. Internal medication can be given to those under 18 only with the permission of a parent. Grandparents, aunts, uncles, brothers, sisters and other friends and relatives cannot give permission for minor children.

There are 10 beds/ cots in the First Aid Station at Disneyland˚ Park and three beds/cots in the First Aid at Disney's California Adventure˚ Park. Folks with disabilities can use the family/companion restrooms in the First Aid Stations. There is a bed/cot in each restroom. They keep a supply of adult diapers in case they are needed.

You are welcome to leave medicine that requires refrigeration at the First Aid Stations. They will keep medical equipment for you as well. Edna kept Lauren's suction machine there since they used it only when Lauren was lying down. You must pick up medical equipment from First Aid before leaving the park each day.

On hot days people with disabilities are welcome to ask for ice packs. The ice packs consist of ice placed in heavy plastic bags.

IF YOU BECOME ILL ON YOUR VACATION

If you become ill and need a physician at your hotel, there is a 24-hour a day service called House Call Physicians available. This service sends physicians to hotels in southern California. At press time, the charge is $270.00 plus the cost of any medication. This service can be reached at 800-362-7911 / 800-DOCS911. Their website is www.housecallphysicians.org. *(Note: this service is NOT connected with Disneyland˚ Resort.)*

DISNEYLAND® WISH LOUNGE

The Wish Lounge is a small room next to the First Aid Station in Disneyland® Park. It is a place where children who are at Disneyland® Resort for

Wish Lounge door

wish trips can lie down or simply go for some quiet. The children and their families can visit the Wish Lounge as often as they like and stay as long as they like. Fresh fruit (apples, oranges and bananas) and crackers are available as well as movies to enjoy.

BABY CARE CENTERS

Disneyland® Park's Baby Care Center is located at the central hub/plaza near the First Aid Station. The one in Disney's California Adventure® Park is near the First Aid Station by the Mission Tortilla Factory. Parents can change diapers, warm baby bottles and baby food. There are two small toilets and there is a room where mothers can nurse their babies.

FAMILY/COMPANION RESTROOMS

There are two family/companion restrooms in each park. In Disneyland® Park they are located outside the Plaza Gardens Stage next to Sleeping Beauty Castle Walkthrough and inside the First Aid Station on Main Street. Over at Disney's California Adventure® Park the restrooms are located next to Flik's Flyers inside "a bug's land" and inside the First Aid Station near the Mission Tortilla Factory.

FASTPASS®

Disneyland® Park and Disney's California Adventure® Park have a system to reduce your time waiting in line for some of the busier attractions. Information about FASTPASS® is printed on the maps to both parks and will be explained here.

FASTPASS® is currently available for the following attractions in Disneyland® Park:

- Space Mountain
- Buzz Lightyear Astro Blasters
- Autopia

FASTPASS machine

- Roger Rabbit's Car Toon Spin
- Indiana Jones™ Adventure
- Big Thunder Mountain Railroad
- Splash Mountain

FASTPASS® in Disney's California Adventure® Park:

- Grizzly River Run
- Soarin' Over California
- Twilight Zone Tower of Terror™
- Mulholland Madness
- California Screamin'

If you would like to ride an attraction that offers FASTPASS® and the waiting line is longer than 30 minutes or so, take your Disneyland® Park or Disney's California Adventure® Park admission ticket and insert it into the FASTPASS® machine/kiosk. You will receive a FASTPASS® ticket with a return time. This allows you to go enjoy other attractions and return during the time on the ticket. When you return, you will enter the FASTPASS® return line and have little or no waiting.

There are a limited number of FASTPASS® tickets issued each day so get yours early in the day. Sue's family used FASTPASS® for Soarin' Over California, Grizzly River Run and Splash Mountain. One day they found FASTPASS® tickets that someone had either lost or tossed and were able to get in more rides on Grizzly River Run. Hang on to those tickets or someone else will get your ride.

Another note about FASTPASS®: at the bottom of your FASTPASS® ticket you can see when you are able to get another FASTPASS® ticket for another attraction. You can get another FASTPASS® as soon as the window of time arrives for your first FASTPASS®, or after two hours of the first being issued, whichever is sooner. Edna and Lauren used timers to remind them to return to attractions. You can also set your cell phone alarm.

PHOTOPASS®

Another nice service Disney offers is PhotoPass˚. They have photographers with high-resolution digital cameras around the parks and they can take photographs of your family, you, your children, etc. They will give you a PhotoPass˚ card, any photos they take of you go onto your Pass. Each time you have them take photos you present them with your PhotoPass˚ card and the new photos are added to the Pass. You can view the photos online at www. DisneyPhotoPass.com and share them at no charge.

Dustin & Mickey Mouse
©Disney Enterprises, Inc.

You can order prints, photo gifts or a CD of your photos online. You can also view your prints and order them at Main Street Photo Supply Co. in Disneyland˚ Park. In Disney's California Adventure˚ Park the PhotoPass˚ center is on the left hand side of Sunshine Plaza after you pass under the Golden Gate Bridge. The photos are available online for 30 days. You can add borders and crop photos online if you wish. The prints are expensive but very professional; you are under no obligation to purchase prints or other photo products because you used PhotoPass˚. It is a nice way to link friends and relatives through photos of your trip to the parks and allow them to purchase a photo if they like. Sue's family used the Disney PhotoPass˚ and was very pleased.

CHAPTER 7
Disneyland® Park Rides

Disneyland® Park is composed of eight areas: Main Street U.S.A., Tomorrowland, Fantasyland, Frontierland, Adventureland, Critter Country, New Orleans Square and Mickey's Toontown Fair. As you enter you will be on Main Street U.S.A, which is based on the Main Streets and Town Squares of much of America. Included in this area are vehicles from the early 1900s, early Disney cartoons, Disney history, shops and places to eat.

Walking along **Main Street U.S.A.** brings you to a central hub where you may choose which land you would like to visit first. To the right is **Tomorrowland**, which is based on futuristic attractions. All the "lands" and areas of the park include eateries and shops featuring gifts based on themes of that particular park. If you enter Disneyland® Park from Downtown Disney® District via the Disneyland® Monorail, you will arrive in Tomorrowland first.

If you proceed straight forward from the Main Street hub, you will enter **Fantasyland** through the Sleeping Beauty Castle Walkthrough. Fantasyland is based on fairytales and fantasy stories. Fairies, princesses and characters from many of the stories visit guests here.

Behind Fantasyland is **Mickey's Toontown® Fair**, which features attractions based on cartoons from Disney characters. You are guaranteed to see Mickey at his house. Minnie is frequently about as are Goofy, Pluto, Chip & Dale and others. The shops and eateries reflect these cartoon characters.

Please note that Toontown generally closes earlier than other parts of the theme park.

If you take an immediate left at the hub you enter **Adventureland**, where as the name implies, adventure awaits. The Jungle Cruise and Indiana Jones™ are some of the biggest hits here, and there is a large shop with adventure clothing and gifts.

A less sharp left turn from the central hub takes you to **Frontierland.** Just like the Old West, there are canoe rides and steamboat rides on the Rivers of America. Other attractions here are a petting "ranch" and the Big Thunder Railroad.

Behind Frontierland and Adventureland are the last two areas of the Disneyland® Park. **New Orleans Square** includes the flavor of New Orleans. Foods and fantasy as well as rides reflect this area of the United States. Pirates and ghosts are the order of the day here in New Orleans Square. Traveling further along the Rivers of America takes you to **Critter Country**, home to Winnie the Pooh and Br'er Rabbit. Rafts to Tom Sawyer's Island, now a Pirate's lair, leave from this area. You will also find Splash Mountain.

MAIN STREET, U.S.A.

A horse-drawn streetcar, horseless carriage and Disney history

Disneyland® Railroad (Main Street Station)

The Disneyland® Railroad at the Main Street Station is not accessible to wheelchair users, ECV users, and those who cannot climb stairs. The stations in New Orleans Square, Toontown and Tomorrowland are all accessible. However, Main Street Station is a good starting point for anyone who is not mobility-impaired.

Handheld Captioning and Audio Description available.

YouTube video http://www.youtube.com/watch?v=BccpSuds0Y0

Disneyland® Story featuring Great Moments with Mr. Lincoln

In this newly revised attraction, an audio animatronic Abraham Lincoln, takes you on a journey through American history.

Guests may remain in their wheelchairs or ECVs for this experience.

Closed Captioning Monitors (preshow only), Assistive Listening (contact a Cast Member for assistance) and Reflective Captioning available.

YouTube videos

http://www.youtube.com/watch?v=Xlp2Mz6cMQ4

http://www.youtube.com/watch?v=z9HQp5C3pvg

http://www.youtube.com/watch?v=k-yd75gEXJ8

Main Street Cinema

This attraction features Disney black and white cartoons shown on six small, simultaneously playing screens inside one room. There are no seats, but there is a railing that guests may lean on. There is also a riser in the center for children to stand on for a better view.

You may stay as long as you like. Guests in wheelchairs may enter by detaching the short rope next to the turnstile.

Main Street Vehicles

Four types of vehicle rides are available on Main Street. These include an old-time Fire Engine, a Horseless Carriage, Horse-Drawn Streetcars and an Omnibus, all presented by National Car Rental. All provide one-way trips down Main Street USA. You may board at Town Square or in front of the Sleeping Beauty Castle in the Central Plaza. The rides are relaxing. The Fire Engine does have a siren and the Horseless Carriages the old "ah hoo ga" sounding horns. You must be able to climb into the vehicle yourself or with the assistance of members of your party. The Omnibus is modeled after a

1920 New York City double-decker bus and accommodates 45 passengers. The Horse Drawn Streetcars can each carry 30 passengers.

> **YouTube video of Fire Engine**
> http://www.youtube.com/watch?v=y6cfzF7xbpo
>
> **YouTube video of Omnibus and Horseless Carriage on Main Street**
> http://www.youtube.com/watch?v=KFU0wkg8NUA
>
> **YouTube video Omnibus**
> http://www.youtube.com/watch?v=D1IiUZe9SSY
>
> YouTube video http://www.youtube.com/watch?v=Y0AdnYh4v6o

TOMORROWLAND

Moving forward into the future, and into outer space

Astro Orbitor

Climb into your own rocket ship for a ride through space. This attraction is like Dumbo the Flying Elephant since "passengers" can raise and lower the height at which they wish to fly. The Astro Orbitors fly faster and higher than Dumbo. You sit one in front of the other for this one and a half minute ride.

Manual wheelchair users and those with Special Needs Passes enter through the regular line. ECV users enter through the exit ramp across from Star Tours and contact a Cast Member. In order to ride you must be able to walk a few steps and climb up and over into your spaceship.

> YouTube video http://www.youtube.com/watch?v=yhqe9agGytg

Star Tours

This is a motion simulator attraction. The ride premise is that you are on a space ride and it is piloted by a robot on his first flight (R2D2 from *Star Wars*). He goes the wrong direction and finds himself in trouble. There are four simulators running simultaneously for this seven minute ride. All four simulators may not be operating when you visit Tomorrowland.

Children must be at least 40 inches tall to ride this attraction. Young children should be accompanied by an adult. *For safety on this ride Disney advises being in good health, free from high blood pressure, free from heart, back and neck problems, not prone to motion sickness and using caution of you have a condition that could be worsened by the ride. Expectant mothers are advised not to ride this attraction. Service animals are not allowed on this attraction.*

Wheelchair users and those with Special Needs Passes contact a Cast Member at the entrance for boarding instructions. There are rows of seats in each simulator. Lauren and Edna have always been directed to sit in the front row, usually near the center, and they found the "jerkiness" that some people have reported "not bad at all."

Guest-activated captioning (preshow only. Please contact a Cast Member for assistance.)

Service animals are not allowed on this ride.

YouTube video http://www.youtube.com/watch?v=cmbGFi016Ac

Space Mountain

Space Mountain is a roller coaster in the dark in which you see realistic stars and galaxies. It is a very popular attraction, so the line is often long for this three-minute-long trip. The ride is smooth and has beautiful views of space, but could be perceived as being "scary" because it is fast moving and in the dark. It is also loud. During the last portion of the ride photos are taken and you can check for these at the end of the exit. There is a charge for the photos.

You must be at least 40 inches tall for this attraction. *For safety on this ride Disney advises being in good health, free from high blood pressure, free from heart, back and neck problems, not prone to motion sickness and using caution of you have a condition that could be worsened by the ride. Expectant mothers are advised not to ride this attraction.*

Wheelchair users and those with Special Needs Passes enter through the exit and follow the arrows to the left. (If you have a FASTPASS® return ticket, go to the entrance and ask a Cast Member for instructions.) A Cast Member takes you to a vehicle in a separate loading/unloading area that allows you to take your time climbing into the vehicle. A transfer seat is available for your use. When you are settled and have your lap bar on, your vehicle is pushed onto the track. When the ride is over, your vehicle returns and is pushed back into the loading area so you may have all the time you require to exit the vehicle.

It can be a bit difficult to climb down into the seats. There is not a lot of legroom, so it is difficult to assist another person to get into the seat.

> **Service animals are not allowed on this attraction.**
>
> **FASTPASS® is an option.**
>
> **Guest-activated captioning (preshow only. Please contact a Cast Member for assistance.)**
>
> **YouTube video http://www.youtube.com/watch?v=-b8XB8SbB9Q**

Disney® Monorail

The Disneyland® Monorail is a transportation system in the sky. You can ride it for fun to see parts of Disneyland® Park or you can use it to get to Downtown Disney® District from Tomorrowland. You can enter Disneyland® Park from Downtown Disney® District and go straight to Tomorrowland. The only stops are Downtown Disney® District and Tomorrowland. The ride allows you to see most of Disneyland® Park and portions of Disney's California Adventure® Park. It actually travels through the Grand Californian Hotel (on the outside).

If you exit Disneyland® Park to enter Downtown Disney® District, you must get your hand stamped to re-enter Disneyland® Park. If you are just exiting the Disneyland® Monorail at Downtown Disney® District and do not leave the Disneyland® Monorail station, hand stamping is not necessary. Downtown Disney® District is not part of Disneyland® Resort and is open to the general public for shopping and entertainment, which is why you must get your hand stamped.

In Tomorrowland, wheelchair users and those with Special Needs Passes use the elevator next to the Winner's Circle and go to the second floor. You operate the elevator yourself. If you are near the submarines you will see a red sign that points you to a very long ramp. You can use the ramp if you like, rather than the elevator.

Once there, you wait for a Cast Member to get a ramp and place it in front of the doorway to your place on the Disneyland® Monorail. Then you wheel right in. Wheelchair users may remain in their wheelchairs while on the Disneyland® Monorail. (Edna's note: Lauren prefers to sit on the regular seat so once in the compartment, I take her out of her wheelchair and sit her on the seat.) There are no wheelchair tie downs, but the ride is very smooth so you don't move around.

Leaving Downtown Disney® District, all passengers must enter the station through a security area where your bags will be checked for unsafe items, glass containers and other things. Wheelchair users and those with Special Needs Passes proceed forward to an elevator that takes you up to the platform where you enter the line for the Disneyland® Monorail. A Cast Member will direct you to a waiting area to board the compartment used for wheelchairs. There is a limit of two wheelchairs per train.

Non-wheelchair users can request a ride in the very front of the Disneyland® Monorail with the driver. The large window on the front brings the sun in so if you have sensitive eyes you may wish to wear sunglasses.

YouTube video http://www.youtube.com/watch?v=2XpUQdwC1l0

Buzz Lightyear Astro Blasters

This very popular attraction is an interactive dark ride that lasts about five minutes. You sit in a ship and use a joystick to turn the ship side to side and in a circle. Each ship has two seats and two laser shooters. You shoot at targets with the laser beams that "hit" targets as you ride along. There is an automatic tally on each ship that keeps track of your score. Some folks like to re-ride this attraction to improve their scores.

Wheelchair users and those with Special Needs Passes enter through the regular line and then proceed through the designated door (marked with the wheelchair access symbol) near the loading zone. There is a wheelchair accessible vehicle available so you may remain in your wheelchair for the ride. People using ECVs must transfer to the available manual wheelchair to utilize the wheelchair accessible vehicle. The wheelchair accessible ship is used only for people who remain in their wheelchairs, so Lauren and Edna were allowed to stay in it and ride as long as they wanted or until someone else needed it. There is a fold-down seat that allows a parent or companion to ride with the wheelchair user.

At the end of the ride there is an opportunity to find a photo of yourself taken during the ride, which you may email home. There is no charge for this service.

FASTPASS® is an option.

Handheld Captioning and Audio Description available

YouTube video http://www.youtube.com/watch?v=VSn9c03BkFc

Disneyland® Railroad (Tomorrowland Station)

To board the Disneyland® Railroad at the Tomorrowland Station, go to the top of the exit ramp and wait behind the yellow line outside the gate. When the train arrives at the station a Cast Member will assist you. You can stay in your wheelchair if you desire. You will sit in the last car on the train; there is limited space available, so you may have to wait for another train.

Autopia, presented by Chevron

This very popular attraction features small cars on a miniature freeway. The cars run on gas so there may be an odor of gasoline in the area. The cars straddle a raised area so you cannot go off the track; you must steer and use a foot pedal to accelerate. The cars travel at a top speed of 7 mph and the ride lasts about five minutes, assuming you don't stall along the way. The cars tend to bottleneck at the end of the ride.

You must be 54 inches tall to actually drive one of the cars. Children at least 32 inches tall may ride with a taller person and help steer while the other rider does the accelerating. The cars do bump into each other occasionally when slower drivers are at the wheel. *For safety on this ride Disney advises being in good health, free from high blood pressure, free from heart, back and neck problems, not prone to motion sickness and using caution of you have a condition that could be worsened by the ride. Expectant mothers and children under 12 months are advised not to ride this attraction due to the bumping.*

Wheelchair users and those with Special Needs Passes enter through the regular line. (If you have a FASTPASS® return ticket, enter the FASTPASS® return line and ask a Cast Member for instructions.) When you reach the tower, go up the elevator. A Cast Member will guide you to an outdoor lift that will take you down to the boarding area. There is a transfer seat available. (Sue's note: Carl used this to get into the car, but it could not be placed in the same position for getting him out. Carl loved steering the car while I used the accelerator. A hand held accelerator is available which Isabel tried, but her hand became fatigued using the device.)

FASTPASS® is an option.

YouTube video http://www.youtube.com/watch?v=AsrzzjZbQsQ

Finding Nemo Submarine Voyage/ Marine Observation Outpost (MOO)

This submarine ride is based on the story of the Disney • Pixar animated feature *Finding Nemo*. The submarines never go completely under water. This 13 minute long ride is highly popular and is a slow loader since all the people have to be out of each submarine before the next group of people can get in. Each submarine has 40 individual seats. Guests climb in and out of the submarines via a spiral staircase.

If you cannot navigate the spiral staircase into the submarine or if you are claustrophobic, there is a Marine Observation Outpost (MOO for short). Anyone is welcome to go into the MOO. You experience the attraction in high definition on a plasma screen. This feature lasts about 15 minutes. There is space for two wheelchairs and there are two benches for others to use. There is standing room as well.

To get to the MOO, go to the regular entrance area, which is near the Monorail entrance ramp, and a Cast Member will take you to the MOO building. You do not need to stand in the line to the actual Submarine Voyage. When you arrive at the MOO, you will have to wait until the previous showing of "*Finding Nemo* Submarine Voyage" is finished; the Cast Member then lets you in and tells you that after a certain point you can leave, if you wish. The show is very loud at times.

> **Handheld Captioning and Audio Description (Submarine Voyage) and Closed Captioning (MOO) available**
>
> **YouTube video of the Submarine Voyage in two parts**
> **http://www.youtube.com/watch?v=1D7QVcj55ts**
> **http://www.youtube.com/watch?v=SzCqZl9NiF4**

Captain EO starring Michael Jackson

Captain EO returns to Disneyland˚ Park. In this 17-minute interactive film, Michael Jackson stars as Captain EO. The film features the music of Michael Jackson and 70mm film and visual effects of Francis Ford Coppola and George Lucas. All guests enter through the regular queue. Guests using a wheelchair or ECV may remain in their chairs for this attraction.

> **Guest activated captioning is available on preshow monitors.**
>
> **Reflective Captioning (contact a Cast Member for assistance), Audio Description and Assistive Listening available**
>
> **YouTube video**
> **http://www.youtube.com/watch?v=T9flCdMQFIg&NR=1**

Starcade

This is a very large and fairly noisy arcade that is wheelchair accessible. The price to play is not included in the Disneyland® Park admission. There are 200 games in the Starcade.

Innoventions

This is a hands-on, walk through attraction that is wheelchair accessible, although you might have to transfer to experience some of the exhibits. Periodically some of the exhibits change. The exhibits are based on life activities such as sports, entertainment, home, school/work, transportation and personal fitness. The attraction shows products that may be available to the general public in the future. You may try out many of the items.

There are two levels in this very large building with no restrooms. Wheelchair users and those with Special Needs Passes enter the lower level through the regular line, which is on a ramp. Use the elevator inside the building to get to the second level. You are free to explore as long as you like.

> **Guest-activated captioning (preshow only)**
> **and Assistive Listening available**

FANTASYLAND

Fantasy stories and fairytales, fairies and princesses

Sleeping Beauty Castle Walkthrough

The Sleeping Beauty Castle Walkthrough is not an attraction one can "ride." It is a beautiful castle that serves as the entrance to Fantasyland. The Castle can be toured by folks who are able to walk through its narrow corridors and up and down stairs. There are dioramas along the way telling the story of *The Sleeping Beauty*. There are some dark areas that may frighten some children. For those who cannot climb stairs and navigate narrow corridors, there is a viewing area on the ground floor of the Castle where you can take a virtual tour of the walkthrough.

Sleeping Beauty Castle serves as a location for many special events and shows. Sleeping Beauty Castle is also a prime photo location. If the crowds at Sleeping Beauty Castle make it difficult to get to Fantasyland, you can go around to the right of the Castle on the route going toward Tomorrowland. You will see the Alice in Wonderland attraction to your left.

A little cement path to the immediate right of the Castle moat leads you to the Snow White Wishing Well and Grotto. If you wait there a little while you will hear the song, "I'm Wishing." If you'd like to make a wish and throw coins into the fountain, you may do so. The coins that are collected are given to various charities.

> **Closed Captioning (accessible experience only)**
>
> YouTube video http://www.youtube.com/watch?v=c_ETvGb_lic

Pixie Hollow

Pixie Hollow is Disneyland® Park's newest character greeting area where you can meet Tinker Bell, Disney's famous fairy. Tinker Bell has her best friends at Pixie Hollow: Rosetta, Iridessa, Silvermist, and Fawn. Pixie Hollow is located in Fantasyland. To find it, veer to your right before crossing over to the Castle and follow the path toward the Matterhorn Bobsleds. Ask a Cast Member for directions if you cannot find the enchanted pathway. Tink and her friends are available for photos.

Peter Pan's Flight

This is a beautiful dark ride in which you sit in a pirate galleon that is suspended a bit above the floor. The perception is that you are flying high over London for about two minutes. Each pirate galleon holds two to three people and has a lap bar that is rather high. Short people can easily bang their faces on the "lap" bar, so hold on. Once you are in the galleon, it stops so the person in the galleon behind you can get out, so be prepared for a little jerking.

In order to get to the pirate galleon, wheelchair users and those with Special Needs Passes enter through the exit, which is to the left of the entrance. You can take a manual wheelchair into the exit, but ECVs have to stay parked outside. Only one wheelchair at a time fits up by the Cast Member. If you need extra time to load, let the Cast Member know and they will give you all the time you need.

Your wheelchair is pretty close to the galleon, so you need to walk only two or three steps. The galleon rocks a little when getting on and off; you have to step up about six inches and over a lip to get in and out. The seats are very low, but there is a lot of legroom. There is a non-skid surface on the floor, but even so Lauren tended to slip a bit during the three downward inclines during the ride. Peter Pan's Flight is a continuous loader; as the occupants of each ship unload, the next occupants get on. (Lauren and Edna's note: We absolutely love this attraction, hailing it as the loveliest one in the park. For us, it is a "never to be missed" attraction. We always ride it twice a day. Sue's Comment: Isabel did not like this because of apprehension of heights.)

Handheld Captioning and Audio Description available

YouTube video http://www.youtube.com/watch?v=KLtyW-e04Kk

Mr. Toad's Wild Ride

This attraction takes you to "Nowhere in Particular." It is a dark ride in an antique looking car. Near the end there are lights that depict a train coming at you, and then you pass through a very warm area.

Wheelchair users and those with Special Needs Passes enter through an access gate to the right of the entrance and wait for a Cast Member to see you. ECVs must be left outside. There is no specially designed vehicle, so Edna could not get Lauren into the car. You have to be able to walk a few steps and get into the vehicle.

> **Caution: Strobe lighting is used on this ride**
>
> **Handheld Captioning and Audio Description available**
>
> **YouTube video http://www.youtube.com/watch?v=j86Eb3toGIM**

Alice in Wonderland

This is a dark ride that takes you weaving back and forth for about four minutes through Alice's adventures. You sit in a caterpillar car that has a front and a back seat. One adult and one child can fit in the smaller front seat. Two adults or three children can fit in the wider back seat. There is no special or modified vehicle for the disabled, although the front seat is slightly easier to get into.

If you need to sit in the front seat and there are only two of you, you will need to go through the line of others waiting and find some "friends" to sit in the back seat to balance the vehicle; this is because there is only one wheel in the front of the vehicle. Any time there are only two people riding, they have to sit in the back seat.

The caterpillars have a non-skid surface on the floor and there is very little legroom. If you or your child cannot readily bend at the knee to 90 degrees while getting in, scoot over while standing and deal with a non-skid surface, you may not be able to get into the caterpillar.

Wheelchair users and those with Special Needs Passes enter through the exit next to the Mad Hatter Store and keep walking until a Cast Member sees you. The Cast Member will tell you where to park your wheelchair. You can stay in your wheelchair to get as close as you need to the vehicle. Once you are out of your wheelchair the Cast Member will move it out of the way. You must remain in your caterpillar until the Cast Member tells you it is time to get out. Your wheelchair will be wheeled close to the caterpillar. Although this is a continuous loader, the caterpillars tend to back up, making it a rather slow loading attraction. (Lauren and Edna's note: We love Alice in Wonderland and consider it a "do-not-miss-and-ride-as-many-times-as-you-can" attraction.)

> **Audio Description available**
>
> YouTube video http://www.youtube.com/watch?v=Eufa1DD3RCE

Dumbo the Flying Elephant

On this two minute long attraction you get to fly in Dumbo and control how high or low you want to go. Guests in wheelchairs and those with Special Needs Passes wait near the exit in a space designated for wheelchairs; a Cast Member will see you.

Lauren on Dumbo ride

There are 16 Dumbos. Two of them, one green and one purple, are specially designed for those who have problems climbing into the standard Dumbos. They each have a door that swings upward so a person can sit on the seat, swivel to get his feet in and slide over. You can take your wheelchair as close as you need in order to get to the Dumbo. A Cast Member takes the wheelchair out of the Dumbo area during the ride and then returns it. This is a slow loading ride since everyone has to be out the exit before the next group can enter.

> YouTube video http://www.youtube.com/watch?v=8XXBG7PDnK0

Casey Jr. Circus Train

This little train seems like a tame little kid ride, but it actually travels rapidly at one point. You see miniature houses, towns and trees along the way. The train is a child-size roller coaster with circus cars and one small circus cage. The cage is difficult for adults to get into and it is very cramped. The last seat is a backward facing one, and on cold days it is the best seat since you won't be facing the wind created as the train moves.

Although there are no specially designed cars, the back seats in the 2nd and 4th cars have lots of leg room, and although it was difficult for Edna to get Lauren into these cars, at least Lauren had leg room. They were given all the time they needed to get on and off. The ride is about three minutes long and is a slow loader since everyone has to be off the train before the next group of people can enter. There are two trains, but the second one is used only during very busy times of the year. If you cannot get on the Storybook Land Canal Boats, this is one way to see the miniature landscapes you would see from the boats.

Wheelchair users and those with Special Needs Passes enter the exit, which is a ramp across from the Village Haus Restaurant. A Cast Member will give you instructions. If you need the second seat in the 2nd or 4th car, let the Cast Member know. Some of the Cast Members do not realize there is much more legroom in those two seats.

> YouTube video http://www.youtube.com/watch?v=0IIIBulrSQ4

Mad Tea Party

This attraction is a spinning ride. Once you've been on the Mad Tea Party ride you will definitely know whether you will be riding it again. Five to six people can fit into each teacup. Each teacup spins individually while moving around on a larger platform. The teacups spin a bit on their own, but

Teresa in a Teacup
(stationary, for photos only)

you can make them spin faster by turning the wheel in the center of each teacup. You can also hold the wheel so the teacup doesn't spin, though it will continue to rotate on the larger platform. Sue and her children all enjoyed the ride and think that everyone should try it at least once, since it is one of the nostalgic Disney experiences.

Wheelchair users and those with Special Needs Passes enter the exit across from the Alice in Wonderland attraction and contact a Cast Member. You can take your wheelchair close to the teacup you wish to sit in and then have someone in your party "park" it along the wall inside the attraction near the ramp to the exit. If it is a manual wheelchair, a Cast Member may move it for you.

It can be difficult for some folks to get into and out of the teacups because the doors are narrow and you have to step up onto the saucer before again stepping up and into the small door, and then sliding under the center turning wheel. This minute and a half attraction is a slow loader. There are 18 teacups, all of which have to be unloaded and everyone has to be out the exit before the next group of people can enter. (Note: Even if you are not prone to motion sickness, you might want to put some time between your meal and this attraction.)

Service animals are not allowed on this attraction.

YouTube video http://www.youtube.com/watch?v=1ijU5dlQPpw

King Arthur Carrousel

This is a lovely carrousel that has 68 horses and one bench. Each horse has a name, and all go up and down in a counter clockwise direction while Disney music plays for this slow, leisurely two minute ride.

To enjoy this attraction, wheelchair users enter through the special entrance to the left of the standard queue where you will be shown to a ramp. You wheel up to a platform that is horizontal to the carrousel. A little "drawbridge" is lowered into place so you can wheel across to the carrousel. You may sit on a bench, sit in your wheelchair in front of the bench or you may ride a horse if you are able. If you choose to get out of your wheelchair, a Cast Member will take it off the carrousel and return it to you at the conclusion of the ride. If you stay in your wheelchair, the Cast Member will lift the center portion of the bench and you will back into this spot. The Cast Member will put blocks in front of your chair's back tires. A person can sit on the bench on each side of the wheelchair.

In the row of horses behind the bench is a horse dedicated to Julie Andrews who rode carrousel horses in the Disney movie *Mary Poppins*. The horse has bells on and is called "Jingles." This is a slow loader since everyone has to be off the carrousel and out the exit before the next group of people enters.

> YouTube video http://www.youtube.com/watch?v=apnxSj8KzSo

it's a small world

This is a very upbeat attraction in which dolls representing many different regions of the world dance while singing, "it's a small world" in their respective languages. While visually stimulating, it is a peaceful ride. This ride lasts 14 to 15 minutes but you will be sitting in the boat longer than that as people load and unload.

Wheelchair users and those with Special Needs Passes go down the ramp to the left of the entrance. You'll be in direct sunlight while you wait. Each boat holds several people.

Wheelchair users can request the boat that has a lift so that you can remain in your wheelchair for the ride. ECV users must transfer to a manual wheelchair available at the attraction. You can step down into a boat if you wish; however, it is a pretty big step with nothing to hold on to.

> Handheld Captioning and Audio Description available
> YouTube video http://www.youtube.com/watch?v=APmHR2bmQgw

Pinocchio's Daring Journey

This is a dark ride lasting about three minutes. You ride in a little woodcarver cart for the story of Pinocchio that begins all nice and cheerful and gradually becomes gloomy. There are areas that may frighten some small children. Near the end of the ride, a big whale opens its mouth at you.

Wheelchair users and those with Special Needs Passes enter through the exit. ECVs must be left outside the exit. The Cast Member will direct you where to wait. There are two specially designed vehicles. Each has a grab bar across the top, in front of the back seat. The side of the seat is hinged and swings around to allow a person to slide across on the seat. There is not much legroom.

Audio Description available

YouTube video http://www.youtube.com/watch?v=-5YNIS8xdfY

Snow White's Scary Adventure

This is a dark ride that lasts about two minutes. You ride in a mining car while you view scenes the story of Snow White and the Seven Dwarfs. A witch that appears a number of times may frighten some small children.

Wheelchair users and those with Special Needs Passes enter through the exit where a Cast Member will direct you where to wait. ECVs have to be left outside. There are two specially designed vehicles, each with a grab bar across the top in front of the back seat. The side of the seat is hinged and swings around, thus allowing a person to slide across on the seat. There is not much legroom.

Handheld Captioning and Audio Description available

YouTube video http://www.youtube.com/watch?v=BkMJnobFLUE

Storybook Land Canal Boats

This is a nice leisurely attraction in which you ride in a boat for seven to 10 minutes while receiving a guided tour of miniature scenes from classic

Disney films. At the beginning of the ride you travel through the mouth of Mostro the Whale.

Wheelchair users and those with Special Needs Passes enter through the exit. The boats are difficult to get in and out of because they rock as you step down into them. Even folks who do not have balance problems can have a tricky time. Each boat holds several people. It is a slow loader since everyone has to be out of the boats and out the exit before the next group enters. There is adequate legroom on this lovely ride. You will be in direct sunlight during this ride. (Edna's note: Lauren loves this ride but I cannot get her in and out of the boat now that she is older because there is virtually nothing to hold onto.)

> **Handheld Captioning and Audio Description available**
> YouTube video http://www.youtube.com/watch?v=aAv1SF3rFS4

Matterhorn Bobsleds

This attraction is a roller coaster type ride in which two cars are connected. There are two tracks used and there is a dispatch time so you have to be able to get in and out quickly. You go up, up, up the mountain and then speed down, in and around the mountain. At the end of the ride you splash into water which is there to slow the cars down, but you hardly ever get wet.

This noisy two and a half minute ride has very sharp fast turns and some dips. You must be 35 inches tall to ride the Matterhorn Bobsleds. Young children should ride with an adult. Each bobsled has room for four people. The person in front sits against the person behind who sits against the seat back.

Wheelchair users and those with Special Needs Passes enter through the two regular lines. When you get near the chalet, a Cast Member will direct you to the accessible entrance area. The only way to enter the bobsled is by climbing over the side and down into it. You might want to walk up to the chalet and ask to look at how folks board before you stand in line. (Sue's note: This was my oldest son Ty's favorite ride. My youngest daughter, Teresa, also enjoys it.) Because you can sit behind a less stable child or adult, the ride is safe and fun. The abominable snowman does make an appearance as you ride and might scare a small child. *For safety on this ride Disney advises being in good health, free from high blood pressure, free from heart, back and neck problems, not prone to motion sickness and using caution of you have a condition that could be worsened by the ride. Expectant mothers are advised not to ride this attraction.*

Service animals are not allowed on this attraction.

Here is a YouTube video that shows both the Tomorrowland side and the Fantasyland side of the ride, running side by side. http://www.youtube.com/watch?v=cfHEeYEXhHs

Disney Princess Fantasy Faire

This is a delightful presentation that offers audience interaction with characters. It may include dancing as well as a maypole dance. Streamers fall from the "ceiling" to the delight of all. You enter through the standard queue and a Cast Member will take you to a lift to reach the main floor. The lift will accommodate only one wheelchair at a time. Sue's three kiddos all had to use it individually. There is plenty of floor area for guests, and the area is covered and cool.

Isabel & Snow White
©Disney Enterprises, Inc.

Outside the Fantasy Faire is an area where you can meet the princesses that are "visiting" and have your photo taken with them. This is organized and you stand in a line (in the shade); the princesses are not rushed and you get to greet about four of them and have individual photos taken if you wish.

YouTube video http://www.youtube.com/watch?v=CnUKksynNmO0

MICKEY'S TOONTOWN

Visit the hometown of your favorite Disney characters

Roger Rabbit's Car Toon Spin

This popular three minute dark ride allows you to spin your taxicab as you travel along. It is more difficult to spin than the Mad Tea Party teacups, and it does not spin automatically. This attraction has some strobe lights and can cause motion sickness if you choose to spin your taxicab. It is quite noisy.

Wheelchair users and those with Special Needs Passes enter the FASTPASS® return line. ECVs must be left outside the attraction. You must be able to get out of your wheelchair and step up into the narrow door of the taxicab within 12 seconds.

Lauren &
Roger Rabbit

> Caution: this ride uses strobe lights.
>
> FASTPASS® is an option.
>
> YouTube video http://www.youtube.com/watch?v=PsNrdWiqa5A

Chip 'n Dale Treehouse

This is a tree house play area with stairs and slides, and children must be able to climb narrow, winding stairs to get inside. Adults do not fit. All guests use the same entrance. There are benches for parents, and if the sun is right, there is shade.

Gadget's Go Coaster, presented by Sparkle®

This cute roller coaster looks really tame but it is wilder than you may think. It is a very short ride—less than one minute. Wheelchair users and those with Special Needs Passes enter through the exit. You must be able to get out of your wheelchair and walk several steps to get into the roller coaster car. There is a lap bar and not much legroom. Children must be 35 inches tall to ride.

Expectant mothers are advised not to ride this attraction.

Service animals are not allowed on this attraction.

YouTube video http://www.youtube.com/watch?v=tJM3DrglLlg

Goofy's Playhouse

This is a play area for children. All guests use the same entrance. There isn't any shade here so you will be in direct sunlight while you watch your children play.

Carl enjoying a moment with Pluto

Minnie's House

This is a walk-through attraction in which you tour Minnie's small house. Minnie strolls around Toontown so she is not always in her house to greet guests. Wheelchair users take the ramp to the right of Minnie's front yard and enter the regular line. Depending on the number of children playing in Minnie's house, you may or may not be able to maneuver your wheelchair around.

YouTube video http://www.youtube.com/watch?v=GYAwphz5AtQ

Mickey's House and Meet Mickey

This is a walk-through attraction in which you see Mickey's house and movie barn. You move along at the pace of the other visitors walking through the house. At the end you get to see Mickey. Each family group and/or small group that is touring together, enters a room where they have some time to meet Mickey and snap photos with him. This is quite nice because you are not fighting a crowd of other people trying to see Mickey Mouse. A Disneyland® Resort photographer is also present if you are using their PhotoPass® system.

The Buchholz Family with Mickey ©Disney Enterprises, Inc

Wheelchair users take the ramp on the right side of the house. Mickey is guaranteed to be in his house.

> YouTube video http://www.youtube.com/watch?v=7fFmlzxyQKk

Disneyland® Railroad (Toontown Station)

Wheelchair users enter at the exit gate near the Disney Princess Fantasy Faire. Stay outside the exit behind the yellow line and wait for a Cast Member to get off the train and assist you when it arrives at this station. You can stay in your wheelchair if you like. You will sit in the last car of the train; there is limited space available.

> **Handheld Captioning and Audio Description available.**
>
> YouTube video http://www.youtube.com/watch?v=BccpSuds0Y0

Donald's Boat

This is a play area for children with things to climb and bells to ring. Children must be able to climb a spiral staircase or the rope ladder in order to be able to toot the whistle. Children have to leave their wheelchairs behind and enter through the regular entrance. They may play as long as they wish while parents sit near a waterfall and watch them.

> YouTube video
> http://www.youtube.com/watch?v=u8UJmB_Il8Q&feature=related

ADVENTURELAND

Adventure in the remote jungles of the world

Jungle Cruise

This is a seven to eight minute boat ride through a jungle. Approximately 25 people ride in each boat. At one point during the ride the captain of the boat shoots a loud gun (blank) at a surfacing hippo. Aware that Sue's

Dustin might be frightened, the skipper warned Sue, who covered Dustin's ears.

Wheelchair users and those with Special Needs Passes enter through the exit. If you can step down a couple steep stairs while maintaining your balance, you can step into a boat. Otherwise, you can ask for the boat

Lauren on the Jungle Cruise

that has a wheelchair lift in it. You then remain in your wheelchair for the boat ride. People with disabilities get on first and get off last. If you cannot reach the brakes of your child's wheelchair or are unable to put on the brakes yourself, ask a Cast Member to do this for you.

Edna's Lauren loves this attraction. One time they saw a live duck sitting on the head of an animatronic hippo going up and down. It was quite funny to watch.

Handheld Captioning and Assistive Listening available

YouTube video http://www.youtube.com/watch?v=LgptOY_s4cg

Indiana Jones™ Adventure

This attraction combines a dark ride with a motion simulator, so as you ride along the track in a military looking jeep you get jostled around; it is quite a rugged, loud, three minute ride with several other people, and can be scary for some children. You must be at least 46 inches tall to ride this attraction. Wheelchair users and those with Special Needs Passes enter through the exit and proceed to the Rotunda until you get to a Cast Member who will give you directions. Lights flicker most of the way. If you use an ECV you will need to transfer to an available manual wheelchair.

You go up the elevator, get out on the second level, go to the next elevator and push #1. If you need your wheelchair until you get into the jeep, let the Cast Member know. You will then need to sit in the front row since your chair won't fit between the uprights that separate the rows of seats. If you don't need your wheelchair up until you get into the jeep, you can sit in any row. You have to be quick stepping up into the jeep and getting the seatbelt on. When the ride is finished and everyone else gets out to the left, wheelchair users will get out to the right. You will then be on your own to operate the elevators.

Edna and Lauren do not consider this ride to be really rough; Sue thought it was pretty rough, but she would ride it again. She loves the *Indiana Jones*™ movies (she thinks Harrison Ford is a hunk). *For safety on this ride Disney advises being in good health, free from high blood pressure, free from heart, back and neck problems, not prone to motion sickness and using caution of you have a condition that could be worsened by the ride. Expectant mothers are advised not to ride this attraction. Young children need to ride with an adult.*

> **Service animals are not allowed on this attraction.**
>
> **FASTPASS**® **is an option.**
>
> **Guest activated captioning (preshow only)**
>
> **YouTube video**
> **http://www.youtube.com/watch?v=R3A6L9tJVxM&feature=fvst**
> **Video is not very clear on the ride as much of it is in the dark.**

Tarzan's Treehouse™

This is a large tree house that has lots of narrow winding stairs. You must be able to walk well in order to climb up and down all the steps. This is a nice way for children who have sensory regulation issues to get in some "heavy work" and might be a nice activity after doing something more stimulating. Everyone enters through the regular line.

There is an interactive show area for folks who cannot walk well or who use a wheelchair. One may access this ground-level attraction by asking for assistance from a Cast Member at the entrance of Pirates of the Caribbean.

> **YouTube video http://www.youtube.com/watch?v=CQF7yR7FRhs**

Enchanted Tiki Room, presented by Dole®

This 15-minute theater presentation has more than 200 audio-animatronic birds, totem poles and flowers that sing. There is a pre-show outside while you wait for the presentation. For children overwhelmed by sensory issues, the show is in the dark and can be loud at times, but it is visually stimulating for children who enjoy lights.

Wheelchair users and those with Special Needs Passes enter through the regular entrance and use the lift located to the right of the stairs. Contact a Cast Member for seating assistance. You may remain in your wheelchair or ECV while enjoying the show.

Assistive Listening Handheld Captioning and Audio Description available.

YouTube video in 2 parts

http://www.youtube.com/watch?v=FlYHEl7jobE

http://www.youtube.com/watch?v=cADh05BF4Ww

FRONTIERLAND

The colorful drama of frontier America

Big Thunder Mountain Railroad

Big Thunder Mountain Railroad is a roller coaster that takes you in a runaway mine train through a mountain cavern for about three and a half minutes. You have to be able to get on and off in 16 seconds because the trains are on a dispatch system. Children must be 40 inches tall to ride and must have an adult with them. Some children, and some adults, too, may find this ride scary and rough. Edna considers this roller coaster to be rather tame, while Sue does not. Sue rode it many years ago and became queasy, while her son, Ty, loved it.

For safety on this ride Disney advises being in good health, free from high blood pressure, free from heart, back and neck problems, not prone to motion sickness and using caution of you have a condition that could be worsened by the ride. Expectant mothers are advised not to ride this attraction.

Wheelchair users and those with Special Needs Passes (with or without a FASTPASS®) go through the exit to the unload area where a Cast Member will give you instructions. There are actually two exits and you can use either one. The #10 train has a special seat on each side. You can get on the #10 train from either exit, and take your wheelchair right next to the train when you get onto the seat. You must be able to board by yourself or with the assistance of members of your party. If an uneven number of trains are running, a Cast Member will take your wheelchair out the exit you entered and down to the other exit to be waiting for you.

Service animals are not allowed on this attraction.

FASTPASS® is an option.

YouTube video http://www.youtube.com/watch?v=6nIMA0gKg6s

Mark Twain Riverboat

On this authentic steam-powered sternwheeler, you take a scenic, relaxing 15-20 minute ride around Tom Sawyer Island on the Rivers of America. There is a recorded narration playing that tells you about the sights you pass. Ducks swim around in the river and some come close to the boat.

Wheelchair users and those with Special Needs Passes use the access gate at the right of the turnstile, or go through the exit of the attraction. Wheelchair users board first and are the last off since the boat is flush with the dock only when empty. Many people ride the Mark Twain Riverboat at the same time. There is a second floor you can go up to if you can climb stairs. This is a really nice ride with no surprises except that the boat horn toots really loudly when leaving the dock.

YouTube video http://www.youtube.com/watch?v=WuETcs3RAI0

Sailing Ship Columbia

This is a full-scale replica of an 18ᵗʰ century merchant ship, the first American vessel to sail around the world. In Disneyland® Park, it sails the same course as the Mark Twain Riverboat. It is not wheelchair accessible. You must climb many very steep steps. If you want to attempt this one, go to the access gate to the left of the turnstile, or through the exit. Edna took Lauren on this when Lauren was smaller and could walk better. The Cast Member sent them up first for safety's sake. While everyone else watched, he remarked that the captain's wife and child were going on first. You will be in direct sunlight for this 15 minute ride and there is no place to sit. It can be crowded and rather noisy on this ship, and the captain narrates as you go.

YouTube video http://www.youtube.com/watch?v=d09ZaQ8AGII

Rafts to Pirate's Lair on Tom Sawyer Island

Wheelchair and ECV users can remain in their wheelchairs and take a round trip ride to the island and back. Wheelchair users enter through the regular line, getting on first and off last via a metal ramp that is placed for you. There is a ramp at the island side as well. The motor is loud and there is no shade on the ride. If you wish to get off and explore the island, many of the pathways are accessible, and there are wheelchair accessible restrooms. There are hills to climb and a rock climbing play area as well as a cave to explore. For kiddos who need sensory regulation and who enjoy climbing, this is an excellent place for them to play.

YouTube video http://www.youtube.com/watch?v=gHU9W7Y9P1k

Big Thunder Ranch

Big Thunder Ranch is a small petting zoo area near Big Thunder Mountain Railroad.

Wheelchair users can go in to pet the animals.

> YouTube video http://www.youtube.com/watch?v=VsI2k07j7co

Fantasmic!

This is a neat special effects show presented on certain nights. Wheelchair users can watch the presentation from a specified area in front of the Golden Horseshoe right down next to the Rivers of America. If you have a problem finding the area, ask a Cast Member. You can ask if there is another viewing area for wheelchair users. You may get wet sitting too close; they will warn you, but be prepared.

> **YouTube videos in three parts**
>
> **http://www.youtube.com/watch?v=8D3wui6xtd4**
>
> **http://www.youtube.com/watch?v=X2AyItJ2slM**
>
> **http://www.youtube.com/watch?v=L8eFRJ1fHyw**

Frontierland Shootin' Exposition

This is an electronic shooting gallery. A wheelchair user can stay in his wheelchair and go up ramps that are located on both sides of the arcade area. Gun positions on the left can accommodate wheelchair users. The price to play is not included in your Disneyland® Park admission.

The Golden Horseshoe Stage

This is a clean-cut dance hall show. Wheelchair users enter through the standard entrance. You need to arrive about 45 minutes early to get a seat at a table. You can order something to eat while you watch the show, although this is not required. The performance is about 30 minutes long, and shows may not be presented daily.

> YouTube video http://www.youtube.com/watch?v=xIfefI5Tjws

NEW ORLEANS SQUARE

Memories of the past, and the promise of the future

The Haunted Mansion

This seven-minute attraction is a ride through a haunted house. It has a lot of special effects which may frighten small children.

From October through December the Haunted Mansion is decorated as Tim Burton's *The Nightmare Before Christmas*. Children will like this because there are large presents and Christmas and Halloween decorations along the way. It is much brighter than the normal Haunted Mansion.

Wheelchair users and those with Special Needs Passes go directly to the entrance; don't get into the line. You will be given a colored piece of paper that explains your special needs. If you cannot walk, you will be given a red piece of paper. You may be asked if you can "transfer." To us, transfer means stand up, pivot and sit down. To the Disney folks, transfer seems to mean get out of your wheelchair and walk in the line. If you cannot walk very far you need to say, "I can't walk." They will give you the red piece of paper that tells Cast Members along the way that you cannot leave your wheelchair until you get right next to the Doom Buggy vehicle, and that the ride will need to be stopped so that you have time to get in and out of the vehicle.

Only three wheelchair and ECV guests are allowed in the mansion at one time.

As you move through the line to enter the Haunted Mansion, there will be a ramp for wheelchair users to the right of the mansion. You will be met along the way by a Cast Member with a flashlight who will direct you to an elevator and show you where to park.

Once you are in the area where you can see the Doom Buggies, you will wait there until a specially designed vehicle comes along. There are 131 Doom Buggies and numbers seven, eight, nine and 10 are specially designed ones. The Doom Buggies look like huge clamshells. The special ones have part of the side cut off so you are able to slide across the seat. Since you know there are 131 Doom Buggies, you can watch the numbers on the sides of the vehicles, which will allow you to prepare.

At the end of the ride when everyone else gets out of their vehicles and onto a conveyor belt and then proceeds out the exit, wheelchair users need to stay in the Doom Buggy and continue back down to where you got on. A green bat on your Doom Buggy will remind the Cast Members not to try to have you get off. The lap bar will rise, but will then fall back into place, so be prepared. When you do get off the ride, you will retrace your steps back to the elevator and wait for a Cast Member to take you back up the elevator and out to the ramp.

> **Handheld Captioning and Audio Description available.**
>
> **YouTube video regular Haunted Mansion**
> **http://www.youtube.com/watch?v=E60nt-_f6Sw**
>
> *Nightmare Before Christmas* **Haunted Mansion**
> **http://www.youtube.com/watch?v=cQ9BjYalvsA**

Pirates of the Caribbean

This is a boat ride in the dark in which you see pirates and Captain Jack Sparrow for about 15 minutes. Each boat holds 15 or more people. Wheelchair users and those with Special Needs Passes enter through the Pirates of the Caribbean exit, to the left of the Blue Bayou Restaurant. Go through the gate to the left. When you first go in your eyes have to adjust to the darkness.

In order to experience this attraction you have to step down into and up out of the boat. It is quite a deep step and there is nothing to hold onto. The Cast Members are not allowed to help guests on and off attractions. Only six physically challenged people at a time are allowed onto this attraction for safety reasons, so you may have to wait up to 45 minutes for a turn to ride. If you have small children or children with sensory issues, be aware that there are two drops at the beginning of this ride and there are some loud noises.

(Sue's note: On our recent trip we noted that the ride had been refurbished with scenes and characters from the *Pirates of the Caribbean* movie. While we were on the ride, there was some sort of mechanical problem and we were stuck at a place where the pirate ship is being attacked by another group. In the boat behind us was a young man with sensory issues/autism who was really having a difficult time with all the stimulation, and with the 15 minute delay in the same spot.)

Service animals are not allowed on this ride.

Handheld Captioning and Audio Description available.

YouTube video in 2 parts:

http://www.youtube.com/watch?v=Ve6KShV1arA

http://www.youtube.com/watch?v=2SReRJUYQSQ

Disneyland® Railroad (New Orleans Square Station)

The front of the train stops near the Haunted Mansion. There is a ramp for folks exiting the train, where wheelchair users wait to board until a Cast Member sees you and comes to get you. The accessible car is the last one, so if it is empty, a Cast Member will motion you up the ramp and to the end of the train. There is a loading platform there that brings you level with the train. The Cast Member will lower a "drawbridge" so that you can cross to the train. The Cast Member will need to know where you plan to get off.

Handheld Captioning and Audio Description available.

YouTube video http://www.youtube.com/watch?v=BccpSuds0Y0

CRITTER COUNTRY

Trail-blaze through country filled with whimsical wildlife

Davy Crockett's Explorer Canoes

This is a person-paddled canoe ride around Tom Sawyer Island on the Rivers of America. The length of the ride varies, but is usually around 10 minutes long. They are real canoes and are not on a track so the ride is a bit different each time.

Wheelchair users and those with Special Needs Passes use a ramp next to the lower level stairs of the Hungry Bear Restaurant to get down to the entrance. You must walk a few feet and maintain your balance while getting into and out of the canoe. There is virtually nothing to hold onto. The seats are relatively close together and they have no backs. They are quite low with very little legroom. When Edna and Lauren rode this, Lauren fell backward onto a gentleman's lap. Lauren was far more comfortable on his lap and he graciously allowed her to stay there. He then carried her off of the canoe at the end of the ride. If you are sensitive to heat or sun, beware that you will be in direct sunlight for the entire ride. This ride closes at dusk.

> YouTube video http://www.youtube.com/watch?v=oYG_41mBBZo

Splash Mountain

This is a flume ride that lasts about 10 minutes. Once you get to the top, you ride down, in and out and around the mountain. The final 52 foot long chute can be scary for some folks. Your photo will be snapped just as you plunge over the top of the chute; you may purchase it at the end of the ride. Wheelchair users and those with Special Needs Passes enter through the exit, which is across from Pooh Corner. Use the same procedure if you have special needs and a FASTPASS° return ticket.

You can take your wheelchair close to the log that you will ride in. You have to walk several steps and then step down into the log and straddle the seat. There is a transfer seat available. It is a little bench seat that can be placed over one of the seats so a person with disabilities can sit a bit higher. The transfer seat helps get a person down into the log, but there is nothing to help that person get out. A gentleman helped get Lauren on and off this ride.

Riders sit in a "line" rather than side by side. Each log has six seats, but two children are allowed to sit together in the wider back seat. Each seat has a back on it. No matter where you sit in the log you may get wet. Sitting in the very front guarantees you getting wet, if not completely soaked. You may consider wearing a poncho if you want to remain dry. They are available at the shop close by. Any items you take with you can also get wet.

For safety on this ride Disney advises being in good health, free from high blood pressure, free from heart, back and neck problems, not prone to motion sickness and using caution of you have a condition that could be worsened by the ride. Expectant mothers are advised not to ride this attraction. Children must be at least 40 inches tall to ride, and those under age eight must be accompanied by an adult.

Service animals are not allowed on this attraction.

FASTPASS® is an option.

YouTube video
http://www.youtube.com/watch?v=0BCIfYc9r8s&feature=related

The Many Adventures of Winnie the Pooh

This attraction takes you on a tour of Winnie the Pooh's Hundred Acre Wood. You ride in a beehive for your three and a half minute trip. Even though the ride is not very long, the lines can be lengthy. While waiting in the line, you may see characters from the Winnie the Pooh stories and can have your photo taken. This helps keep squirmy kids entertained. Once you get under the trees, there is intermittent shade.

Wheelchair users and those with Special Needs Passes enter through the regular line. If you are using an ECV, you will need to transfer to a manual chair (available for your use) or walk through the line. There is a (manual) wheelchair accessible beehive, which means that your wheelchair can go right into the beehive vehicle. The wheelchair accessible beehive vehicle is very clever and Cast Members call it "The Wave." No one could tell Edna why it is called "The Wave." Every time Edna and Lauren rode it folks in line exclaimed, "Wow, that is NEAT!!" and it is. Part of the vehicle rotates to allow the person in the wheelchair to roll onto the vehicle without needing a ramp. Once the brakes on the chair are set (by you), the Cast Member puts a block behind the rear wheels to prevent the chair from shifting. A Cast Member then rotates the vehicle frontward. There is a very high "lap bar," and a small seat behind the wheelchair for the user's guest.

Edna recommends that you be sure to get the wheelchair front tires against the front of the car and that the Cast Member gets the block tightly against the back tires to diminish the jerking that occurs as the ride stops and starts to let other guests onto the attraction. Edna and Lauren were allowed to ride multiple times since this vehicle is used only for guests using wheelchairs and goes around empty if no one needs it.

> **Handheld Captioning and Audio Description available**
>
> **YouTube video http://www.youtube.com/watch?v=VGJIpa_ZXug**

CHAPTER 8

Disney's California Adventure® Park Rides

Disney's California Adventure* Park is just that: exploring attractions and rides that highlight the State of California. As you enter Disney's California Adventure* Park for the first time, you will want to check in at the Guest Relations Lobby for information regarding the accessibility of the park's attractions. A Cast Member can issue Special Needs Passes and answer any questions you may have. The Guest Relations Lobby is to the immediate left of the turnstiles upon entering before passing under the Golden Gate Bridge. As you enter the park you will pass under Disney's California Adventure* Park's Golden Gate Bridge and will be facing the **Sunshine Plaza.**

If you veer to the right and then proceed forward around Sunshine Plaza you will be on a pathway that circles the Grizzly River Run attraction. Just off to the left of this pathway is **"a bug's land."** This area is fashioned after the Disney movie *a bug's life.* The rides and other attractions feature bugs from the movie. The rides are designed with smaller children in mind, although of course children and adults of any age may ride. There is a water play area as well.

If you take the first right as you face Sunshine Plaza, you will find yourself at the **Golden State** area of Disney's California Adventure* Park. This area highlights California's natural wonders. You will find Soarin' Over California to your right. This attraction it is one of the most popular in

Disney's California Adventure® Park, so you may want to try FASTPASS® right away so you are sure of experiencing this ride. The pathway winds over to Grizzly River Run and the Redwood Creek Challenge Trail. If you are staying in Disney's Grand Californian Hotel®, you may enter Disney's California Adventure® Park from the hotel and you will be in this area of the park.

As you follow this path you will eventually come to a "fork in the road" where you may choose to go straight across a bridge and enter the **Paradise Pier** area of Disney's California Adventure® Park or you can continue to the right and visit **Paradise Pier** from the opposite direction. **Paradise Pier** highlights California's beaches.

If you travel to the left as you face Sunshine Plaza you enter **Hollywood Pictures Backlot**. This area highlights California's film industry.

SUNSHINE PLAZA

The Sunshine Plaza plays host to a continually changing venue of entertainment. Check the *Entertainment Times Guide* to see which shows and parades will be available.

"a bug's land"

Life from a bug's point of view, based on Disney• Pixar's movie, a bug's life

It's Tough To Be a Bug!

This is a humorous 3-D show as seen through the eyes of bugs. You will wear 3-D glasses. The theater will be dark at times and there are many special effects. Some children may be frightened. The film lasts eight to 10 minutes. (Sue's note: Dustin refused to wear the 3-D glasses. This doesn't ruin the show, however.)

Everyone enters through the regular line. Wheelchair users then ask a Cast Member where to position themselves for the show.

> **Reflective Captioning, Assistive Listening
> and Audio Description available.**

Flik's Fun Fair

This amusement park "constructed by bugs" appeals especially to younger children, while adults will enjoy the creative "bug's view."

Heimlich's Chew Chew Train

This attraction is a miniature railroad in which you ride slowly in Heimlich the caterpillar. Heimlich talks as he takes you for the ride. Children, especially, will enjoy this two minute long ride.

Wheelchair users enter through the regular line and must be able to get out of their wheelchairs and into Heimlich. There is a specially designed accessible seat (number 7). During the ride you go under a piece of watermelon and through a watermelon smelling mist. When you go by the cookies you smell cookies.

> **YouTube video http://www.veoh.com/videos/v658138hQsmapNB**
>
> **YouTube video http://www.youtube.com/watch?v=4hBktEBNrSE**

Tuck and Roll's Drive 'Em Buggies

This is a small version of bumper cars that look like pill bugs. Two people (the size of one adult and one child) can fit into each car. You must be 35 inches tall to ride and you need to be able to press on the floor pedal to make the car go and be able to steer the steering wheel.

Everyone enters through the regular entrance. A specially designed vehicle is available on this ride, but you must be able to transfer into the car. It is a noisy area. *For safety on this ride Disney advises being in good health, free from high blood pressure, free from heart, back and neck problems, not prone to motion sickness and using caution of you have a condition that could be worsened by the ride. Expectant mothers are advised not to ride this attraction.*

> **Service animals are not allowed on this attraction.**
>
> YouTube video http://www.youtube.com/watch?v=YIAb80TRZmc

Flik's Flyers

In this one and a half minute balloon type ride, you sit in square baskets that look like food containers; they gently fly around a center pole. There is a special basket for those who cannot get into the narrow door of the other baskets – it is the Casey Jr. animal cookie box. The door is cut differently so a person can sit, pivot their feet into the basket and simply slide over on the seat.

Everyone enters through the regular line. The Casey Jr. special basket stops near the entrance. Wheelchair users can take their wheelchair to the basket. A Cast Member will move the wheelchair to a safe place while you are flying. This is a slow loading ride since everyone has to be out the exit before the next group of folks is allowed to board.

> YouTube video http://www.youtube.com/watch?v=Gd-u4nvw3hA&NR=1

Francis' Ladybug Boogie

In this minute and a half ride you sit in little ladybugs that spin like the teacups in Fantasyland. Everyone enters through the regular line. There is one ladybug in which part of the seat turns 180 degrees. You sit on the special seat which is then rotated back to the normal position. You can take your wheelchair to wherever the special ladybug happens to stop; a Cast Member will move your chair out of the way.

> YouTube video http://www.youtube.com/watch?v=9XC6cyS-3Ms

Princess Dot Puddle Park

This is a water play area that is entirely accessible. It is an open area where you can explore and get wet at your own pace. It has two parts, separated by greenery. The water shoots from the ground through drains and jets to other drains. There is a huge watering can from which a mist of water cascades down. There are benches to sit on while children play. Children must wear shirts, shorts and shoes while playing, but swimming suits are okay. If you plan to visit this area it is a good idea to take extra clothing and a plastic bag for wet items. On hot days this is a nice place to sit since the water seems to cool the immediate area temperature.

There is a Family/Companion Restroom near Princess Dot Puddle Park.

YouTube video http://www.youtube.com/watch?v=qoGMsIwwgJQ

GOLDEN STATE

The Golden State area takes you to visit five fabulous areas of California: Grizzly Peak, Condor Flats, Pacific Wharf , The Bay Area and the Golden Vine Winery (Napa Valley). There are no rides in the Bay Area or Napa Valley.

Grizzly Peak

California state wilderness areas

Grizzly River Run

This attraction is a white-water raft ride. If you don't mind getting wet, this is the adventure for you. Edna and Lauren said they did not get wet. Each circular raft holds eight people. You will float down the river and then will be pulled up a 50-foot incline. You then ride down the white water as your raft turns and bounces off the sides of the river, goes through caves and down a couple of drops before the last major drop. Because the rafts turn as they are floating down the rapids, no one seat can count on being dry. Ponchos are available for purchase or you can bring your own, if you really don't want to get wet. Lockers are available for keeping your belongings dry (like cameras and cell phones).

Everyone enters through the regular line. If you have a FASTPASS® return ticket, enter the FASTPASS® return line. Wheelchair users proceed to the designated gate that has an access symbol on it (Sue's kids call this "the blue wheelchair access guy"). Enter the gate and go down the dock and wait for a Cast Member. The Cast Member will bring a raft over for you to board. You must be able to get out of your wheelchair or ECV and step down two steps into the raft. You are allowed all the time you need getting in and out of the raft. This is a very popular attraction with long lines (depending on the weather).

You must be 42 inches tall to ride Grizzly River Run. Young children should be accompanied by an adult. Each passenger in the raft wears a seat belt. Sue's daughter, Anna and niece, Veronica really enjoyed this ride. Teresa also enjoyed it. Anna and Teresa had no trouble staying in the raft even though they do not have arms and cannot hang on. *For safety on this ride Disney advises being in good health, free from high blood pressure, free from heart, back and neck problems, not prone to motion sickness and using caution of you have a condition that could be worsened by the ride. Expectant mothers are advised not to ride this attraction.*

> **Service animals are not allowed on this attraction.**
>
> **FASTPASS® is an option.**
>
> YouTube video http://www.youtube.com/watch?v=8vLRmhLIsLk

Redwood Creek Challenge Trail

This two-acre adventure play area has rivers, hollow logs, caves, cliffs, trails, water crossings, and many stairs. You may see characters from *"Brother Bear."* The area also features an amphitheater where you can watch a show called, "The Magic of Brother Bear."

Enter through the regular line for this attraction. You will be given a map that shows the accessible trails, and you proceed at your own pace.

....
Assistive Listening available (Ahwahnee Camp Circle)

YouTube video http://www.youtube.com/watch?v=tTja_ybxzLc
A small boy experiencing parts of the trail including the rockslide, rock climbing wall and a "suspended" crawl-through tunnel.

YouTube video http://www.youtube.com/watch?v=QmgaODd6Zjk
This gives you the "flavor" of the more challenging aspects of the Challenge Trail. It strikes Sue as the perfect area to allow children with sensory challenges and those with high activity levels a chance to do some "heavy work." There are a lot of places for a proprioceptive workout including a springy ropes course, a climbing wall and lots of stairs.
....

Condor Flats

California's aviation industry

Soarin' Over California

This attraction is an incredibly realistic ride that makes you feel like you are flying (in a seated position) over California. This attraction uses an Omnimax screen, a gentle breeze and the faint smell of oranges to transport you into the scenes. There is one point in which you dip down into an orange grove, and people have instinctively lifted their feet to avoid hitting the trees. At another point, not to spoil the fun but in case you have a child who might "freak out," there is a golf ball that comes at you and some people duck to miss it.

You must be at least 40 inches tall to ride this attraction; young children should be accompanied by an adult. There is a spot marked on the back of the seats and if your head does not reach this spot, you must use the extra strap between the legs.

Wheelchair users and those with Special Needs Passes enter through the regular line unless you have a FASTPASS˚, which allows you to enter the FASTPASS˚ return line. Once you are inside the building there are steep ramps to and from the loading area. Proceed to the seating area and ask a Cast Member for boarding instructions.

Wheelchair users can take their wheelchair as close to the seat as they need. A specially designed vehicle is available. You must be able to get out of your wheelchair and transfer to a seat. A Cast Member or a member of your party will move your wheelchair to the side. After the lights go off, the seats are lifted into the air, row by row. (Sue's note: Carl and I absolutely love this ride. Isabel kept her eyes closed for most of the flight and held onto my arm.) *Disney's precautions include fear of heights and motion sickness.*

Service animals are not allowed on this ride.

FASTPASS® is an option.

Guest-activated captioning (preshow only)

YouTube video http://www.youtube.com/watch?v=_D2G6xAje8E

The video also shows the pre-flight video if you want to see that information ahead of time. Don't let this video dissuade you from riding, as the feeling you get from this ride truly cannot be conveyed by the video. You might not want to watch the whole video if you don't want to "spoil" the fun.

Pacific Wharf

Monterrey's Cannery Row and San Francisco's Fisherman's Wharf

Mission Tortilla Factory, hosted by Mission® Foods

Everyone enters the door to stand and watch a video of how tortillas are made. Guests may remain in their wheelchair or ECV. After the short video you then push a door open. You enter a room where you are offered a tortilla. They make potato tortillas and corn tortillas; whichever tortillas are being made that day are the ones you will be offered. You do not have to accept one.

> Guest-activated captioning monitors and
> Assistive Listening available (preshow only)
>
> YouTube video http://www.youtube.com/watch?v=EoMPUDJclJE
> This is a video of children being given the history of tortillas.

The Bakery Tour, hosted by Boudin® Bakery

Everyone enters a room to stand and watch how Boudin sourdough bread is made. In the next room you take a self-guided tour. The large windows are 28 inches from the floor so wheelchair users can see how the bread is baked. You can watch for as long as you wish. Samples of bread are not available.

> Guest-activated captioning (preshow) and Assistive Listening available
>
> YouTube video http://www.youtube.com/watch?v=aEG5VGr4Ius

Bountiful Valley Farm!

This is an educational play area accessible to everyone where you can stay as long as you wish. There is huge farm equipment to climb on and a large irrigation water play area. The object of this area is to learn about farming in California.

PARADISE PIER

A lake, a waterslide, and more screamin' fun

King Triton's Carousel

This attraction is a carousel featuring elaborate sea creatures. For this approximately two minute ride, wheelchair users may remain in their wheelchairs, sit on a bench or ride a sea creature. If you are using an ECV you must leave it behind and transfer to the available manual wheelchair. Wheelchair users enter through the entrance to the right of the regular line. You get onto the carousel via a ramp and "drawbridge."

This is a slow loading ride since everyone must be out the exit before the next group can go into the attraction. Lauren and Edna were allowed to ride as many times as they wanted since there was not any other wheelchair user who needed the bench.

Jumpin' Jellyfish

This is a parachute-type attraction that raises you up and gently lowers you to the ground. It is a calm ride designed for children. There are two Jumpin' Jellyfish areas in one, with six seats in each, making 12 parachutes all together. Two people can sit on each ski-lift type seat. Everyone riding this one-minute ride must be at least 40 inches tall.

Everyone enters through the regular line. Wheelchair users can take their wheelchairs right next to the seat. The seats are 31 inches from the ground and there is a pommel between the legs on each seat, with an upright pipe between the seats that serves as a "hand hold."

This is a slow loading ride since everyone has to be out the exit before the next group of riders is let into the loading area. Service animals are not allowed on this ride.

Maliboomer

This attraction takes you straight up, 180 feet, in four seconds. Once at the top you experience zero gravity. You are then lowered and raised until you are safely on the ground.

Riders must be at least 52 inches tall to experience this attraction. *For safety on this ride Disney advises being in good health, free from high blood pressure, free from heart, back and neck problems, not prone to motion sickness and using caution of you have a condition that could be worsened by the ride. Expectant mothers are advised not to ride this attraction.*

(Sue's note: when Anna was younger, she got on this ride before I could stop her. I was afraid she would fly off the ride since she doesn't have arms. Anna was safe, although maybe not so sound after the ride. I was a wreck! This attraction is not for the faint of heart or for their mothers.)

Everyone enters the regular line and once at the loading area, wheelchair users ask a Cast Member for boarding instructions. You must be able to leave your wheelchair, walk to the seat and get onto it. This attraction may not operate during inclement weather.

> **Service animals are not allowed on this attraction.**
>
> **YouTube video**
> **http://www.youtube.com/watch?v=Z3hA2C3AQrc&feature=related**

Mulholland Madness

This exciting one and a half minute ride is the Disney style "mad mouse" in which up to four people sit in one automobile type vehicle. You are taken on a track that has sharp turns, making you feel as though you will fall off the edge around the corners. Edna and Lauren thought it was really jerky and did not enjoy the ride. Sue's son, Carl, absolutely loved it. Some strong men lifted him into the vehicle. The track goes uphill at the beginning, then goes down in increments. There are three small roller-coaster-like dips. Edna warns that the ride comes to a sudden and complete halt at the end of the ride without slowing down. This throws people forward without warning. You must be at least 42 inches tall to ride.

Everyone enters through the regular line unless you have a FASTPASS˚, in which case you enter the FASTPASS˚ return line. The entrance and exits are ramps. Wheelchair users must leave their wheelchairs and walk to, then climb into, the vehicle. This attraction may not operate during inclement weather. *For safety on this ride Disney advises being in good health, free from high blood pressure, free from heart, back and neck problems, not prone to motion sickness and using caution of you have a condition that could be worsened by the ride. Expectant mothers are advised not to ride this attraction.*

> **Service animals are not allowed on this ride.**
>
> **FASTPASS˚ is an option.**
>
> **YouTube video http://www.youtube.com/watch?v=97lJUCsIkJ0**

Golden Zephyr

This attraction is a swing type ride in which up to 12 people sit in silver rocket ship cars. Two people can sit in each seat while you swing around a central structure. This three minute long ride is shut down for safety reasons when it is windy.

Everyone enters through the regular entrance. Wheelchair users then take the elevator to the second floor. On the second floor door will open to your left. A Cast Member will guide you to your car. You must be able to get out of your wheelchair and get into your flying rocket ship. There is one special seat on car number two that comes down "for easier access." Ask a Cast Member about this option. The Cast Member will move your wheelchair when you are seated and return it to you at the conclusion of your ride.

YouTube video http://www.youtube.com/watch?v=HvtPNHMVaPI

Silly Symphony Swings

This attraction will be "new" sometime in 2010. The old Orange Stinger is in the process of being completely renovated and will be a large open swing that spins and tilts. The story line is inspired by a 1935 cartoon in which Mickey Mouse directs an orchestra that gets out of control. As the music becomes "wilder," so does the ride.

Guests must be between 40-48 inches tall to ride in a tandem swing with a responsible person. Guests shorter than 40 inches cannot ride this attraction. You must be able to transfer from your wheelchair or ECV to the swings.

Mickey's Fun Wheel

This is a very large Ferris wheel that has both swinging and stationary gondolas. If you want to ride in a swinging gondola enter through the regular line. At the split, go to the left entrance. If you prefer a stationary gondola enter through the exit. If you are a wheelchair user, you may ride in your wheelchair on the ride. If you use an ECV, you will need to transfer to a regular wheelchair available at the ride. You may also sit in the regular seat. The swinging gondolas are on a track, and as the Ferris wheel goes around, the gondolas slide on the track giving one a thrilling but incredibly unstable feeling. Good for loads of screams. This video shows how the swinging gondolas move down the track. This attraction may not operate during inclement weather.

YouTube video http://www.youtube.com/watch?v=0eXsMuXFnco

S.S. Rustworthy

This is a sunny playground for children themed as a shipwrecked fireboat. There are fountains that spray, so children will get wet and possibly soaked. You may wish to pack swimsuits and sunscreen when the weather is warm. You may stay as long as you like. All ages can play on S.S. Rustworthy. There is a very loud bell that children love to clang, water spray, water cannons, and surfboards to balance on. The S.S. Rustworthy area is wheelchair accessible.

YouTube video http://www.youtube.com/watch?v=malUlOhLJoI

California Screamin'

This attraction is a roller coaster that makes a 360 degree upside down turn in front of Mickey Mouse's head. A voice counts down from four to one; you are then thrust from zero to 55 miles per hour in five seconds. Anyone riding this approximately three minute long ride must be at least 48 inches tall. This ride may cause motion sickness and is not for the faint of heart.

For safety on this ride Disney advises being in good health, free from high blood pressure, free from heart, back and neck problems, not prone to motion sickness and using caution of you have a condition that could be worsened by the ride. Expectant mothers are advised not to ride this attraction.

The seat backs are high to support the heads and necks of most folks. This is a very intense ride that has a soundtrack that includes screaming (the riders also scream!!). From a point on Paradise Pier you can look down at the beginning of this ride and watch it take off at break neck speed and listen to the real screams.

Wheelchair users enter through the regular line unless you have a FASTPASS˚, in which case you enter through the FASTPASS˚ return line. You then go to the elevator. A specially designed seat is available.

> **Service animals are not allowed on this ride.**
>
> **FASTPASS˚ is an option.**
>
> YouTube video http://www.youtube.com/watch?v=upHZ2ptl3WA

Games of the Boardwalk

The price of these games of skill is not included in your admission. The games cost about $2.00 each.

Toy Story Mania!

Toy Story Mania! is an interactive ride in which you wear 3-D glasses and play midway-type games while you ride along on this four and a half minute attraction that features characters from Disney• Pixar *Toy Story* movies. Three of the games are breaking plates, ring toss and balloon popping. All of the games are on screens and you use toy cannons to do the shooting. At the end you are given a score to show how well (or not) you played.

The vehicle turns you toward each of the games. The ride is attractive inside, bright and loud, with photos of huge toys/characters on the walls.

The regular vehicles each have two seats with two people in each seat, back to back. Each pair of people has their own cannon. To experience *Toy Story* Mania! everyone uses the regular line. Wheelchair users can remain in their wheelchairs because there is a wheelchair accessible vehicle for you. ECV users must transfer to the available manual wheelchair. The special vehicle has room for a wheelchair and one other person. There is a ramp so you can get into the vehicle. The lap bar can be removed and one can just use the seat belt. The vehicle is off to the side so you have all the time you need to get in and out.

The 3-D glasses are sanitized each night. You do not have to wear the 3-D glasses if you'd rather not. Flash photography is not allowed on this ride.

> **Guest-activated captioning available (preshow only)**
>
> **Hand-held Captioning available**
> **(please visit Guest Relations for this device)**
>
> YouTube video http://www.youtube.com/watch?v=wUjbI_P0k6E

HOLLYWOOD PICTURES BACKLOT

Visit the backlot of a Hollywood film studio

Disney Animation

There are three shows that feature aspects of Disney animation: "Animation Academy," "Sorcerer's Workshop," and "Turtle Talk with Crush" (the turtle from Disney • Pixar's film *Finding Nemo*). It is totally accessible. There are also walk-through exhibits of Disney animation from numerous movies. This is a fascinating exhibit for art enthusiasts and budding young artists.

> **Guest-activated captioning, Assistive Listening (preshow)**
>
> **Audio Description available for "Turtle Talk with Crush"**

Disney's *Aladdin*—A Musical Spectacular

This is a 40-minute live musical performance of *Aladdin*. Wheelchair users can go through the regular line. Ask a Cast Member for help with seating if you need it. YouTube has the entire performance available in seven parts.

> **Assistive Listening available.**
>
> YouTube video http://www.youtube.com/watch?v=FbZtHOxceSA

Muppet*Vision 3D

Muppet fans will enjoy this 3-D show. Enter through the regular line, and once in the theater ask a Cast Member where to position yourself in your wheelchair. There is a large waiting area with a pre-show available that can entertain you while you have some down time.

> **Guest-activated captioning (preshow)**
>
> **Reflective Captioning, Assistive Listening and Audio Description available**
>
> YouTube video http://www.youtube.com/watch?v=VhVEVukWMe8
> (They should have put the 3-D glasses on their camera)

Playhouse Disney – Live on Stage!

This is a 20-minute interactive show that features characters from *Mickey Mouse Clubhouse, Handy Manny, Disney Little Einsteins™* and more. Enter through the regular line and proceed to the theater entrance. Ask a Cast Member where to position yourself in your wheelchair for the show. Edna and Sue did not see this production. It appears from the following YouTube video that one sits on the floor to watch the performance.

> **Guest-activated captioning (preshow only) and Assistive Listening available**
>
> YouTube video http://www.youtube.com/watch?v=sr-NwdhwQEE

Monsters, Inc. Mike & Sulley to the Rescue!

This is very cute; even if you haven't seen Disney • Pixar's film *Monsters, Inc.* you can follow the story line. Everyone enters through the regular entrance. When you get to the taxi ride vehicles, wheelchair users will be taken to the left. The taxis go really close to the platform so you can get into the taxi. If you are using a wheelchair, you will be instructed to back into the taxi. This will be easy as two seats have been removed for this purpose. There is a seat for one companion. Edna reminds you to make sure the brakes on the wheelchair have been locked. ECV users must transfer to the available manual wheelchair. A Cast Member will place a "block" in front of the back tires to keep the wheelchair from moving forward as the rides stops and starts at the beginning and end of the ride.

There are 17 vehicles total. The ADA (Americans with Disabilities Act) vehicle is only for those who need it for their wheelchairs. Edna was told they could ride again until another person in a wheelchair needed the vehicle. Two things to be aware of are bright lights and a low siren noise.

> **Handheld Captioning and Audio Description available**
>
> YouTube video http://www.youtube.com/watch?v=ZU6MD-dL81g

The Twilight Zone Tower of Terror™

In this attraction you find yourself in an old hotel. If you are a wheelchair user or have a Special Needs Pass, enter through the regular queue, or if you have a FASTPASS*, enter the FASTPASS* return line. You will first go into a library to learn about the story line of the hotel. Once you leave the library you follow the line to go to your elevator. There are three elevators. Some people go up the stairs to enter the elevator higher up. Wheelchair users always go into the library to the right. Wheelchair users need to be in line six.

Wheelchair users will sit in a front seat that has no barrier in front of it, so one has space to transfer. You will be given all the time you need. A Cast Member or a member of your party can move your wheelchair out of the area. A Cast Member makes sure everyone is wearing a seat belt on this ride. A barrier is moved in front of the aisle and once the door is closed you are backed up into the actual elevator. You go up once slowly, then up to another floor slowly and then the fun begins. You go up and down very smoothly. Each time the ride is a bit different because a computer generates random sequences.

You go up to the very top floor, the 13ᵗʰ, and have your picture taken. After a couple more ups and downs you again go to the 13ᵗʰ floor, from where you can actually see the park. You do a couple more ups and downs, getting a feeling of being weightless for a few seconds before the ride ends. Lauren and Edna loved it.

You must be 40 inches tall to ride. Young children might be afraid due to the darkness, and should be accompanied by an adult. *For safety on this ride Disney advises being in good health, free from high blood pressure, free from heart, back and neck problems, not prone to motion sickness and using caution of you have a condition that could be worsened by the ride. Expectant mothers are advised not to ride this attraction.*

Service animals are not allowed on this ride.

FASTPASS˚ is an option.

Guest-activated captioning (preshow only)

YouTube video http://www.youtube.com/watch?v=r1J_c1EkKzQ

CHAPTER 9

Planning for the Child who has Autism or Sensory Integration Issues

MANAGING THE ANTICIPATION

Many of these ideas will work with young children in general. If your child will drive you "crazy" or "crazier" by repeatedly bugging you with the "are we there yet?" type of compulsive chatter, you might want to consider just how long you can bear this excitement, and keep the trip a secret until you are closer to the date you leave. Bear in mind, of course, that it is fun to have something exciting to anticipate. Small children and some children with developmental issues cannot really gauge time. Using a special calendar with a picture of a favorite Disney character on the date you will leave home or arrive in California might help. Cross out the dates until you leave.

For some children who might not understand calendars, you could try the paper chain with links that you remove one by one, daily, until you reach a picture of Mickey.

PLANNING FOR THE DISNEY EXPERIENCE

For children who do not do well in new or overly stimulating environments, you could try any of the following:

Familiarize yourselves with the world of Disney

Read Disney story books or watch Disney movies so they will recognize favorite characters and storylines.

Order your Free Disney Parks Vacation Planning DVD which includes Walt Disney World® and Disneyland® Resort with tours of Disneyland® Park, Disney's California Adventure® Park and their resort hotels at https://www.disneyvacations.com/dv/en_US/VacationPlanningDVD/index?sourcecode=15949&hdrType=default&vcnType=dlr&referrer=dlr&bhcp=1. The DVD is available in English and Spanish and takes 2-3 weeks to arrive. (Sue notes that she ordered one online and it arrived in three days, so you never know.) If you register at this site (free) you can enjoy online games, promotions and see behind-the-scenes videos of Disneyland® Resort.

Try using the Interactive Maps of Disneyland® Park and Disney's California Adventure® Park on YouTube

The Disneyland® Resort maps that are on their website are not as good as Disney's print maps. More interesting and interactive maps are available at YouTube for

Disneyland® Park at http://www.youtube.com/watch?v=cuH2nBarrrw and for Disney's California Adventure® Park at http://www.youtube.com/watch?v=BWQ8sgx_os0. You are invited to click on any "land" or area and a new interactive map of that land will appear with opportunities to click on any attraction, which will show you a video of that attraction. Generally there is music and the videos of each ride or other attraction are quite good. To return to the previous map from the attraction videos simply hit the back arrow on your computer screen.

Maps and Picture Boards

If you have a nonverbal child, making a communication board with photos of characters and rides ahead of time could help your child greet and request. We have a free print-it-yourself picture communication board at our blog at http://Disneylandwithdisabilities.wordpress.com.

The Disneyland® Park and Disney's California Adventure® Park printed maps are nice for the drawings of rides. You could request a map ahead of time and laminate it for use as a communication board. (Disneyland® Park and Disney's California Adventure® Park have separate maps, so ask for both) by phoning a personal assistant at 714-781-7290.

STRUCTURING YOUR VISIT

If you need to have more structure while you are at Disneyland® Resort you can go online to the Disneyland® Resort Monthly Calendar and Daily Entertainment Calendar. Disneyland® Resort Monthly Calendar has the hours that Disneyland® Park and Disney's California Adventure® Park are open for the entire current month listed: http://disneyland.disney.go.com/disneyland/en_US/calendar/monthly/monthly?name=CalendarMonthlyPage

The "Daily Entertainment Calendar" has the scheduled entertainment for a couple of months at a time listed by dates. It may be possible to choose a special activity for each day that will be your child's priority choice for that day.

For children who like to act out stories with toys, there is no shortage of Disney toys and characters available almost everywhere, including used at second hand and thrift stores. For a child who likes to "fidget" with something in their hands, a small plastic Disney character might be great to have along.

One parent wrote online that her family went to great lengths prior to their vacation to help their three-year-old son who had verbal and physical dyspraxia. They wrote social stories for him with pictures of the transportation they would use, airport terminals, shuttles, planes, the place they would stay and the pool there. They researched the Parks. They brought little containers of bubbles like party stores sell for weddings, and used them for long waits in line. They brought a water mister bottle to keep cool. They only wished they had brought a Step-by-Step device to record a greeting like, "Hi. My name is _____" so their son could "talk" to/greet the characters. (Find Step-by-Step, a small recordable communication device, in the Resource section.)

SOCIAL AND SENSORY STORIES

Write your own social stories. Social stories are stories for children who may need to learn how to cope with new and sometimes challenging environments and be able to interact socially with other people in new situations. Social stories can be about transportation you will be using to get to your destination, the hotel where you will stay, how to greet a character at Disneyland˚ Resort, how to shake hands, or any number of possible activities that could be overwhelming to a child. To find information on what a social story is and how to write one for your child, go to http://www.polyxo.com/socialstories/introduction.html#whatare. There are many free printable social stories online. Search "free printable social stories."

Children who have difficulty processing sensory input on an ordinary day, may need a lot of support to enjoy all aspects of Disneyland˚ Resort. Children can have sensory processing issues with any of the senses. You can write sensory stories for your child that includes coping mechanisms tied into the theme of your vacation. For information on sensory stories see the following websites:

http://www.sensorystories.com/

http://www.sensorystories.com/About.aspx

http://www.sensorystories.com/Instructions.aspx

http://www.sensorystories.com/FAQ.aspx

Or to purchase a sensory story about Standing in Line, see:

http://www.theraproducts.com/index.php?main_page=product_therapro_info&products_id=321162

RESOURCES & TIPS FOR CHILDREN WITH SENSORY PROCESSING ISSUES

These companies carry a wide variety of items for children and adults with sensory processing difficulties:

http://www.integrationscatalog.com/

www.southpawenterprises.com

For children who have strong aversions to smells, you could try bringing an odor that the child does like to "cover up" offensive odors. Aromas are available in spray cans, essential oils, lotions and even scented candles (don't light a candle at Disneyland° Resort). As a physical therapist, Sue used coffee grounds between other aromas children were exposed to at the clinic, to "erase" the previous odor, before helping a child address a new aroma.

For children who are very sensitive to light, you could try hats you can pull down over the eyes or sunglasses.

For the child who is sensitive to loud noises, earplugs or earmuffs might just do the trick. Headphones with pleasant sounds or music the child enjoys may help you get through some of the noisier attractions. Noise-canceling headphones and earbuds do not completely cancel loud noises, but let you listen to music at a decreased volume.

For the child with taste issues or food texture issues, you may need to pack foods the child will eat. You can send foods and snacks ahead to your hotel and then bring them with you into Disneyland° Resort so your child isn't trying to deal with too many new things at once. There are many fast food and other food establishments surrounding Disneyland° Resort and the area's hotels. We all need healthy food that we enjoy while we are on vacation. Please also see information about the Disneyland° Park and Disney's California Adventure° Park restaurants and food carts in Chapter 6.

If your child is touch sensitive, you may want to get him used to any new clothing you want him to wear on vacation. Pre-washing the items, removing tags and allowing the child to get used to them at home may go a long way toward making him comfortable with new apparel. The same goes for shoes for the whole family. As mentioned earlier in the book, it is estimated that people walk six or more miles per day in the Disney Parks; better to have comfortable shoes and socks that are "broken in."

If your child does not like being "bumped" or brushed against by children at school and these occasions result in altercations, you will need to be proactive. If the child is young and would not mind riding in a stroller or rented wheelchair, you could try that to allow him some space so he is not jostled continually by crowds and long lines of waiting children and adults.

For the child with sensitivity to movement, you may want to look at the ride video links we have included in Chapters 7 and 8 to see how each ride looks. Some people cannot tolerate spinning movements like the Tea Cups but tolerate the Carousels. Some people do not like heights, but enjoy rides on the water. Edna and Lauren loved the Twilight Zone Tower of Terror™ with its dropping elevators, but Edna does not like Ferris wheels. Fortunately, Mickey's Fun Wheel was being refurbished when they were at Disney's California Adventure® Park.

COPING STRATEGIES WHILE ON VACATION

Be sure you have a Special Needs Pass (see Chapter 6). This will help you avoid situations that your child cannot handle. If you notice your child becoming agitated and losing control of himself, try to remain calm yourself and you will be more likely to come up with the coping strategies your child already uses or you use with the child on a regular basis. Giving a child some joint approximations while you are in a line or tight space, pushing down on their shoulders while they are standing or giving very firm hugs and squeezes can be very "centering" for some children. If your child uses a weighted vest or blanket or uses clothing designed to give proprioceptive feedback, you may need to have those items with you for support. Have your child carry his own backpack (with padded straps, of course) and weight it with some drinks. For proprioceptive garments see: http://www.spioworks.com/

Both Disneyland® Park and Disney's California Adventure® Park have places for open-ended types of play. Areas for free play, climbing and sliding that allow the child to "run off steam" or to get some "heavy work" accomplished are scattered throughout the parks. The Redwood Creek Trail in Disney's California Adventure® Park has some easy rock wall areas and some climbing and bouncing pathways and lots of stairs that go up to the lookout tower.

If your child has a bedtime routine at home, it may be helpful to continue this in the strange bedrooms of hotels. A favorite blanket, toys or DVDs will allow the child to "chill out" a bit and have something familiar.

Also, returning to the hotel during the day for a break from the stimulation may help. For many children, swimming is calming and gives much proprioceptive feedback and a heavy workout.

SAFETY

For safety considerations, this information from earlier in the book is repeated.

Lost Guests

If your child is lost, he will be taken to Lost Children which is next to First Aid in Disneyland° Park and is next to the Baby Care Center in Disney's California Adventure° Park.

Medical Information

If you or your child has a serious medical condition, Medic Alert° has bracelets, necklaces and wallet cards you can carry with you. An emergency number to access your medical information is available in case you are unable to provide it yourself. http://www.medicalert.org

Wandering Children

If you have a child who is prone to wander, My Precious Kid at http://www.mypreciouskid.com has shoe tags and also temporary tattoos that you can use with a marker to list your phone number. They also have a clip-on teddy bear (plastic) that emits a 86-db sound when activated by a key chain the parent carries, should a child wander away. They have a number of practical kid products and a special needs section as well.

Resources

COMFORT AND SAFETY PRODUCTS

My Precious Kid for shoe tags, temporary tattoos that you can use with a marker to list your phone number, sound devices to keep track of a wandering child and other child safety products: http://www.mypreciouskid.com/ID-shoes-tags.html

Step-by-Step by AbleNet
http://www.spectronicsinoz.com/product.asp?product=27773

Umbrellas for the wheelchair. Consider getting an umbrella for the wheelchair to keep hot sun off child/adult. Edna's umbrella resources follow: http://www.sammonspreston.com/Supply/Product.asp?Leaf_Id=553668. This umbrella is large, but even though they state that the stem is adjustable it is NOT. http://www.redwagonsonline.com/Product.aspx?pid=37 This is the one we use although we have to use two of them since they are small. It has a good strong clamp, and near the clamp it can be bent in any direction.

Two other sites with clip-on umbrellas:

One Step Ahead (also has many unique and useful baby products), http://www.onestepahead.com/catalog/product.jsp?productId=534674&cmSource=Search

For those with odor sensitivity or allergies: Please see the last page in Resources for a sign in English/Spanish that you may post in your hotel room to ask that no sprays be used. You can either tear the page out or copy it.

GENERAL TRAVEL INFORMATION FOR FOLKS WITH DISABILITIES

Barrier Free Travels (Candy Harrington's Weblog)
http://barrierfreetravels.com/serendipity/

FAA information for passengers with disabilities
http://www.tsa.gov/travelers/airtravel/specialneeds/index.shtm

Medic Alert® medical ID tags, necklaces and bracelets http://www.medicalert.org

PACKING LIST RESOURCES

Extensive travel tips http://www.essortment.com/in/Travel.How.To/index.htm

Disney World® Ultimate Packing List
http://www.mousesavers.com/timeismoney.html#packing

Specific packing lists for kitchen, emergency, car rides, water parks etc.
http://www.themouseforless.com/downloads/trip/UltimatePackingList.shtml

A to Z packing list http://www.allearsnet.com/pl/pack.htm

"Lists of Everything" compiled by a number of contributors
http://www.mousebuzz.com/forum/travel-tips/30864-danas-super-packing-list.html

Simplify your carry-ons http://www.tsa.gov/assets/pdf/311_brochure.pdf

ONLINE DISABILITY INFORMATION ABOUT DISNEYLAND® RESORT

Disney's *Guidebook for Guests with Disabilities* (a 32 page e-book)
http://aDisneyland.disney.go.com/media/dlr_v0200/en_US/help/disabil_gdebk_3_08.pdf

For Disney guests with impaired mobility http://adisneyland.disney. go.com/media/dlr_v0200/en_US/help/Mobility1.pdf

For Disney guests with hearing impairments http://adisneyland. disney.go.com/media/dlr_v0200/en_US/help/HearingDisability1.pdf

For Disney guests with visual impairments http://adisneyland. disney.go.com/media/dlr_v0200/en_US/help/VisualDisability1.pdf

Service animals http://adisneyland.disney.go.com/media/dlr_v0200/ en_US/help/ServiceAnimal1.pdf

Lighting effects
http://adisneyland.disney.go.com/media/dlr_v0200/en_US/help/Lighting1.pdf

GENERAL ONLINE DISNEYLAND® RESORT INFORMATION

Introduction to Disneyland® Park
http://www.mouseplanet.com/tag/dlintro.htm

Introduction to Disney's California Adventure® Park
http://www.mouseplanet.com/tag/dcaintro.htm

FASTPASS® information
http://disneyland.disney.go.com/plan/guest-services/fastpass/ Not all rides are listed, but it tells how to use FASTPASS˙.

Disney's online ticketing prices:
http://disneyland.disney.go.com/tickets/

VIDEOS OF DISNEYLAND® RESORT ATTRACTIONS

Here is a link for people who want to see inside the Castle:
http://www.yesterland.com/sbwalkthru.html

This is a YouTube walk-through of the Castle:
http://www.youtube.com/watch?v=DQ5n0g1CK9M

Many of the rides at Disneyland® Resort have been filmed by visitors and put on YouTube. http://www.youtube.com/results?search_query=Disneyland+rides&search_type=

"Flik's Fun Fair," a review by a mom of a four year old and a 17 month old. http://www.mouseplanet.com/akrock/ak021007.htm

DISNEYLAND® PARK AND DISNEY'S CALIFORNIA ADVENTURE® PARK PICTURE COMMUNICATION BOARDS

"Picture Communication Boards" of Disneyland˚ Park and Disney's California Adventure˚ Park rides for guests who have limited verbal skills are on our blog and may be printed free of charge. http://Disneylandwithdisabilities.wordpress.com

"PLEASE DO NOT SPRAY IN ROOM" SIGN

Please do not spray deodorizer in this room.
People in this room have severe allergies.

Por favor, no spray deodorizer en esta sala.
La gente en este cuarto tiene alergias severas.

Please leave this note on the mirror.

Por favor deje estas notas en el espejo.

Index

BUY A SHARE OF THE FUTURE IN YOUR COMMUNITY

These certificates make great holiday, graduation and birthday gifts that can be personalized with the recipient's name. The cost of one S.H.A.R.E. or one square foot is $54.17. The personalized certificate is suitable for framing and will state the number of shares purchased and the amount of each share, as well as the recipient's name. The home that you participate in "building" will last for many years and will continue to grow in value.

Here is a sample SHARE certificate:

YES, I WOULD LIKE TO HELP!

I support the work that Habitat for Humanity does and I want to be part of the excitement! As a donor, I will receive periodic updates on your construction activities but, more importantly, I know my gift will help a family in our community realize the dream of homeownership. **I would like to SHARE in your efforts against substandard housing in my community!** *(Please print below)*

PLEASE SEND ME _____ SHARES at $54.17 EACH = $ $_____

In Honor Of: _____

Occasion: (Circle One)   *HOLIDAY   BIRTHDAY   ANNIVERSARY*

       OTHER: _____

Address of Recipient: _____

Gift From: _____   *Donor Address:* _____

Donor Email: _____

I AM ENCLOSING A CHECK FOR $ $_____ PAYABLE TO HABITAT FOR HUMANITY **OR** PLEASE CHARGE MY VISA OR MASTERCARD *(CIRCLE ONE)*

Card Number _____ Expiration Date: _____

Name as it appears on Credit Card _____ Charge Amount $ _____

Signature _____

Billing Address _____

Telephone # Day _____ Eve _____

PLEASE NOTE: Your contribution is tax-deductible to the fullest extent allowed by law.
Habitat for Humanity • P.O. Box 1443 • Newport News, VA 23601 • 757-596-5553
www.HelpHabitatforHumanity.org